Concerning English Administrative Law

Concerning English Administrative Law

By SIR CECIL THOMAS CARR

NEW YORK
COLUMBIA UNIVERSITY PRESS
1941

COLUMBIA UNIVERSITY PRESS, NEW YORK

Foreign agents: OXFORD UNIVERSITY PRESS, Humphrey Milford, Amen House, London, E.C. 4, England, AND B. I. Building, Nicol Road, Bombay, India; MARUZEN COMPANY, LTD., 6 Nihonbashi, Tori-Nichome, Tokyo, Japan

MANUFACTURED IN THE UNITED STATES OF AMERICA

To L. and O. R.

Preface

THE SIX chapters of this book reproduce six lectures delivered upon the Carpentier foundation at Columbia University in the fall of 1940.

They discuss various aspects of public administration in Britain. The first recalls what may perhaps be described as England's New Deal of the eighteen-thirties; this beginning of novel relationships between central and local authorities, and between both sets of authorities and the people, created problems of what is vaguely called "administrative law" which are with us still. The stresses have varied with the times. In 1929 a brilliantly written attack was launched in England against the "new despotism" in a phase of reaction from the intensive system of government developed during and after the last war. The well-informed criticisms came from so high a source that they could not be ignored. The Lord Chancellor, as is well known, invited a strong committee to examine the scope and exercise of ministers' powers and especially the alleged or suspected encroachment of the executive upon the functions of the legislature and the judiciary. Two of the six lectures deal with delegated legislation and with the judicial work of governmental agencies in the light of the committee's report. Its reasonably reassuring conclusions may have failed to reach the whole of the audience which was startled by the sounding of the alarm.

Another lecture reviews the laws with which Britain has armed herself in the present crisis. A fifth deals with the form and publicity of the written laws in general; the important topic of legislative drafting is one to which Sir Courtenay Ilbert drew attention in his Carpentier Lectures in 1913 and to which Columbia University has made its own notable contributions. The final lecture contains some fugitive observations upon bureaucracy, a term which, whether seriously or playfully applied, betokens a certain contempt. Citing the famous sentence in the Massachusetts Bill of Rights, Woodrow Wilson remarked that governments were always governments of men, "and no part of any government is better than the men to whom that part is entrusted." If we want to improve administration and administrators, we must not always be deriding them.

To Dr. Nicholas Murray Butler, President of Columbia University, who honoured the series of lectures by introducing the first of them in person, I am grateful for this and other kindnesses. I have also to thank other distinguished members of the University for presiding on subsequent occasions—Professors Young B. Smith, Dean of the Faculty of Law, Lindsay Rogers, Joseph P. Chamberlain, Noel T. Dowling, and Walter Gellhorn. To them and to other friends, old and new, I am indebted for far more help than I have managed to acknowledge. A lecturer is not an essayist. The traces of oral delivery, the inadequate documentation, and the excessive use of the first person singular have not been deleted from the following pages in the process of converting the spoken into the printed word. Certain anxieties occurring in that process have been happily removed by the skill and patience of Miss Ida Lynn and others of the Columbia University Press and by the speed and intuition with which Miss Helen Kline transcribed a palimpsestic manuscript.

In a classic French comedy a character is asked if he knows Latin. "Yes," he replies, "but please proceed as if I did not." A visitor, groping for American parallels to familiar English instances, must either confess his ignorance or dissemble it like Monsieur Jourdain. Yet the fundamental differences between the United States and Britain in constitutional structure and in geographical scale cannot obscure the community of history and outlook. To both countries government, tolerated as an unfortunate necessity, is but the means to the end; to both countries the end is liberty.

C. T. CARR

Columbia University
December 5, 1940

Contents

1. The Eighteen-Thirties and After

I think we ought not only to admit but to welcome every improvement in the organisation of local and subordinate authority which, under the unquestioned control of Parliament, would tend to lighten its labours and to expedite the public business.—MR. GLADSTONE'S ADDRESS TO THE ELECTORS OF GREENWICH (1874)

JUST about a hundred years ago a British foreign minister had to explain to the young Queen Victoria a newfangled word which no girl of eighteen in the year 1838 would be expected to understand. It was the hybrid and abusive term "bureaucracy." People who live in islands cannot help being insular; with an insular complacency, of which I dare say you all have your favourite examples, Lord Palmerston felt able to assure the Queen that bureaucracy was a phenomenon exclusively continental. That was true enough in the context in which he was writing. But, as we now look back to the eighteen-thirties, it seems odd that Palmerston should have ignored the activities on the home front at that very moment of one whom good judges have since regarded as the arch-bureaucrat of all time in Britain.

Edwin Chadwick, though his father lived the latter half of his life in New York and though his sister married an eminent American lawyer, may not in himself be a character to excite your special interest; but his wonderful pioneer work in public health in England and his carrying on of the Benthamite tradition into living memory certainly deserve the biography which has not yet been properly written, and justify, I hope, my using him today as an introductory figure. He was a great investigator of social conditions, a great writer of bluebooks, and a great sanitary reformer. One modern historian has attributed to him the vices as well as the virtues of the official mind —rigidity, ruthlessness, a certainty that he was right, and a conviction that his opponents represented merely "sinister interests." [1] Another has written of him that, born in 1801 in a Lancashire farmhouse where the children were washed all over every day, he made it his life's object to wash the people of England all over every day by executive order.[2] Let us dwell rather upon his virtues. He was seized when young with what he called the "sanitary idea"—the idea that unhealthy conditions produced disease, and disease produced poverty. When he was not busy with other crusades, such as pensions for teachers, public promenades, physical training for trade unionists, and employers' liability for blameless accidents (our workmen's compensation of today), he was devoting himself to every kind of sanitary research and improvement, whether it was housing, sewerage, water supply, prevention of epidemics, disposal of the dead, registration of the causes of death, or the cure of intemperance. At the age of eighty-six, when he wrote a vigorous essay advocating the use of tricycles by the police, he pointed out that not

[1] E. L. Woodward, *The Age of Reform* (1938), p. 434.
[2] G. M. Young, *Victorian England*, II, 422.

only would the constables thus have the legs of the criminals but they would also find tricycling a valuable sanitary exercise. When he died in 1890, a post-mortem examination would surely have revealed that word "sanitary" graven upon his heart.

Chadwick's early writings on mortality statistics and preventive police attracted the attention of James Mill, the father, John Stuart Mill, the son, and the great Jeremy Bentham himself. Over eighty, failing in health and eyesight, but still toiling at his *Constitutional Code,* Bentham took the young Chadwick into his house as literary secretary and bequeathed to him a legacy and a library as well as those theories of centralization and paid officialdom which the disciple was to translate into practice. The year of Bentham's death was the year of the passing of the Reform Bill, the revolution of 1832 rounding off the revolution of 1688. The new Parliament (and its successors), impulsive, rather undisciplined, and very serious, knew that the country expected it to experiment and to risk the impact of State interference upon individual liberties. A series of non-party royal commissions and committees explored social conditions; their disclosures shocked public opinion and revealed the gap in the local administration of those times between efficient government in some places and scandalous neglect in too many others. Parliament, fortified by the reports and recommendations of these exploratory bodies, gave a smooth passage to several controversial Bills which were in no way the product of the government machine. And so Britain got a quick and quiet revolution in the laws of factories, poor relief, municipal corporations, prisons, and presently public health, while striking changes were also being made in civil procedure and summary jurisdiction and mitigation of savage punishments. This reinforcement of the governmental process by a concentration of the intelligence of men of independent mind, not always attached either to Parliament or to political parties, is an object lesson to which our eyes turn in these no less stimulating times.

Chadwick was in the forefront of several of these reforms. In 1833 he was serving on two royal commissions—poor laws and factory laws. He soon showed his exceptional skill in handling facts and figures and his fertility in suggestions. He must have some of the credit for what is usually called Lord Shaftesbury's factory law of 1833,[3] which substituted four centralized and paid factory inspectors for an earlier provision whereby local justices of the peace appointed one justice and one clergyman to supervise the health and morals of apprentices in the local cotton mills. The amateur inspection by the justice and the clergyman had been useless; they seldom inspected at all, and never at night; they usually gave notice of their visit in advance. He had an even bigger share in the great Poor Law Amendment Act of 1834,[4] which created a temporary central Poor Law Board of three. The board was given the widest power of making rules and orders for the management of the poor—delegated legislation on matters of principle, not merely on matters of supplementary detail. There was to be uniform supervision

[3] 3 & 4 Will. 4, c. 103.

[4] 4 & 5 Will. 4, c. 76.

from the centre in place of the previous system of sporadic and haphazard orders made by what Chadwick's report described as "over 1500 local authorities unskilled and practically irresponsible, liable to be biased by sinister interests." During the drafting conference on the Bill somebody suggested a right of appeal from the decisions of the commissioners. Lord Althorp said it was an absurd idea; the appellate court, whether consisting of judges or the Secretary of State or the Privy Council, would be quite incompetent to deal with the issues involved. The Act, however, did eventually provide that rules, orders, and regulations should be removable by certiorari into the King's Bench court. In one of its annual reports the Poor Law Board observes that the courts interpreted this jurisdiction strictly.

Chadwick, although this comprehensive scheme of poor law reform was largely of his own devising, had the mortification of not being made a member of the board. He was not quite consoled when he was appointed secretary and told that although the salary was less the power would be greater. I fear he was neither the ideal secretary nor even a loyal civil servant. He quarrelled with his masters, and on one occasion he denounced them publicly. In 1839 he ceased to attend their meetings; after 1841 he did not even go to the office. His absence does not seem to have broken their hearts; perhaps they were happy to think of him writing bluebooks elsewhere. In 1838 he had been appointed to another commission, this time to investigate the need of a preventive police; the report led to legislation in the following year. He inspired a medical inquiry into fever in London and generally into the sickness and mortality of the poor, himself distributing seven thousand copies of the report. He had pulled strings till his Poor Law Board was directed to inquire how far the causes of disease in London prevailed elsewhere. His own report in 1843 on the sanitary condition of the labouring classes is a landmark in public health, and, by way of encore, he added an extra volume on the practice of burials in large towns. There came a set-back in 1847. Parliament refused to prolong the temporary Poor Law Board of three. Few people loved what by this time had been called the three Neros, the three pashas, the three fiends incarnate, and the Pinch-Pauper Triumvirate of Somerset House. Many people plainly did not mind what happened to the board so long as Chadwick lost his job. It was a significant story of plans excellent on paper but lacking the practical criticisms which Parliamentary control would have provided. It was a good idea to classify paupers and segregate them in different institutions—the able-bodied men, the able-bodied women, the old people, the children, the sick, and the feeble-minded. Chadwick was laughed at for proposing to found an "idiotopolis." It was complained that his plan worked so rigidly that husbands and wives of whatever age were parted at the workhouse door and parents were forbidden the sight of their children. Clergymen said such a law was un-Christian, not meet to be obeyed. Disraeli called him a monster in human shape. Next year, largely as a result of Chadwick's researches and reports, Parliament (stirred perhaps by a series of disastrous epidemics) created a General Board of Health, somewhat on the lines of the late Poor Law Board. Chadwick was appointed to this new body. One of his late masters opined that perhaps it would keep him quiet. That was too optimistic. There is a characteristically Chadwickian statute of 1850, which, while placing the regulation of metropolitan burials under the General Board of Health, incidentally so centralized the management of London funerals that Whitehall could even appoint the chaplains and make contracts with undertakers for burials at standardized rates for all classes and with railways for carrying coffins and mourners and so on.[5] After two years of this intrusion of the State into the most intimate part of the lives of the people, the Act was repealed and those provisions which were conspicuously in advance of public opinion were superseded.[6] Then in 1854 the General Board of Health itself came to an end. Chadwick and an official department had gone down together for the second time. His enemies called him doctrinaire, a centralizer, an interferer with property rights, an enemy of the people. Burke tells us that it is not given to mankind to tax and to please any more than to love and to be wise. Equally, we may add, it is not given to a man to be a sanitary reformer and to be popular. Chadwick retired on a not inadequate pension of £1,000 a year, and there for the moment we may leave him. The ultimate revival and development of specialized departmental agencies in England is too long a story to re-tell here.

This introductory excursus on Chadwick, which I have

[5] 13 & 14 Vict. c. 52.

[6] 15 & 16 Vict. c. 85.

been inflicting upon you at disproportionate length, has revealed certain aspects of that vaguely named administrative law which I have hitherto evaded the duty of defining. There they were, in full view, a century ago—central government replacing a loose local administration, the paid professional official superseding the unpaid amateur, delegation of the legislative power, the possibility of appeal from administrative decision, the strictness of judicial interpretation, the well-intentioned bureaucrat's outpacing of public opinion, and so on. Most of the modern criticisms of bureaucratic encroachment were, as Dr. Chih-mai Chen has so admirably shown us, audible in the eighteen-thirties.[7] How modern it all is! Whether this English outburst of centralization has any exact parallel in American experience and, if so, at what period are questions which a visitor can leave to the scholars of that university which bred up Alexander Hamilton.

Inspired perhaps by recent events and experiments in France, Jeremy Bentham had encouraged these phenomena in England. In doing so he encouraged the change from the medieval view of statute law. The Middle Ages, I suppose, had thought of a statute as either a mere declaration of the unchanging common law or else as a quite exceptional instrument. In the modern theory (or at any rate the modern practice) statutes are the ordinary day-by-day machinery of State interference designed to bring the greatest happiness to the greatest number—a roseate vision presented to the eyes of politicians by the widening of the franchise. How the Benthamites could

[7] *Parliamentary Opinion of Delegated Legislation* (1933), pp. 71, 76.

reconcile that theory with their natural addiction to the doctrines of *laissez faire* is one of the puzzles of political science.

The disciples who sat at Bentham's feet must have learnt two principles—uniformity of administration throughout the country and the impossibility of achieving it without a large increase in the activity of the central government. Legislation was useless without some means of enforcing it. Uniformity, the element which attracts and collects executive rules and orders into the legislative rather than the administrative class, was much in the air in the eighteen-thirties. Those four central factory inspectors under the 1833 Act were to meet in conferences at least twice a year and to make their proceedings, rules, orders, and regulations "as uniform as is expedient and practicable." The royal commission on the poor law recommended in 1834 that the new Poor Law Board's regulations should "as far as may be practicable, be uniform throughout the country." The new provision for county police forces in 1839 declared the expediency of uniformity in the rules for the government, pay, and clothing of the police. The legislature promoted uniformity because the medieval arrangements of local administration were no fit instruments for the policy of social improvement which the country was understood to be demanding. Uniformity meant centralization. Railway development, the invention of the electric telegraph, and the introduction of penny postage lent their aid. Naturally this novelty of centralization was stoutly resisted. In the debates on the Poor Law Amendment Bill a noble peer opposed this scheme which had no English name. It was so continental. The French system of centralization, he said, was inconsistent with the genius and incompatible with the prosperity of England. Two years later a bishop denounced "the vice of modern legislation, 'centralisation' as it is called, a word not more strange to our language than the practice is foreign to our ancient habits and feelings." The Benthamite policy of "inspectability" nevertheless marched on. The eighteen-fifties saw the beginning of a civil service recruited by competitive examination.[8]

We nod approvingly today when someone tells us that, whereas the State used to be merely policeman, judge, and protector, it has now become schoolmaster, doctor, housebuilder, road-maker, town-planner, public utility supplier, and all the rest of it. The contrast is no recent discovery. De Tocqueville observed in 1866 that the State "everywhere interferes more than it did; it regulates more undertakings, and undertakings of a lesser kind; and it gains a firmer footing every day, about, around and above all private persons, to assist, to advise and to coerce them."[9] Nassau William Senior, a Benthamite ten years older than Chadwick, a colleague of his on the original Poor Law Commission, had justified this tendency. A government, he thinks, must do whatever conduces to the welfare of the governed (the utilitarian theory); it will make mistakes, but noninterference may be an error too;

[8] For comments by Chadwick on the low standard of officials appointed by patronage see p. 155, below.

[9] *Oeuvres,* III, 501.

one can be passively wrong as well as actively wrong.[10] One might go back much earlier still to Aristotle, who said that the city-state or partnership-community comes into existence to protect life and remains in existence to protect a proper way of living. What is the proper standard? That is an age-long issue which is still a burning question of political controversy. The problems of administrative law are approached in the light of that fire. Those who dislike the statutory delegation of legislative power or the statutory creation of a non-judicial tribunal will often be those who dislike the policy behind the statute and seek to fight it at every stage. On the one side are those who want to step on the accelerator, on the other those who want to apply the brake.

Before I go further, may I mention certain differences between the British and the American scene, certain insular peculiarities which you will know how to discount if they seem to colour what I say?

We should be convinced in England that the temporary Poor Law Board and General Board of Health—with each of which Chadwick fell—failed because they offended against the British principle of ministerial responsibility. Not being represented in Parliament, "the tyrants of Somerset House were without a Minister either to control or defend their masterful proceedings." [11] As the historians have put it, these magnificent early efforts were partially wrecked by the reformers' excessive zeal,

[10] Marian Bowley, *Nassau Senior and Classical Economics* (1937), p. 265.

[11] G. M. Young, *Victorian England*, p. 461.

which was untempered by regard for the stage of development of public opinion. "Had they been subjected week by week to Parliamentary questioning, their course would have been impeded; but delayed reform, even when slow and hesitant, is preferable to extreme activity followed ere long by rebellion and stagnation of work." [12] By ministerial responsibility I mean responsibility of Ministers to Parliament, the legislator's power to drag ministers' doings into the light of day not merely by a full-dress vote of censure or by discussion on the estimates or criticism of government policy in debates on the Consolidated Fund Bills but also by the opportunities on motions for the adjournment of the House of Commons and above all by the highly developed technique of Parliamentary questions. A glance at the reports of House of Commons proceedings will show how successfully grievances are ventilated by the adroit and pertinacious interpellation administered by private members. Do not let me seem to be belittling by comparison the power of Congress to keep the executive up to the mark, the power of holding the purse strings, the power of demanding information, obtaining periodical reports and conducting investigations, the power of criticism on the floor of the House and that formidable if perhaps rusty blunderbuss of impeachment, which is kept in the constitutional cupboard on both sides of the Atlantic. But in the United States the executive means a single head with a fixed term of office, whereas in Britain ministerial responsibil-

[12] Sir A. Newsholme, *Ministry of Health* (1925), "Whitehall series," p. 86.

ity, pressed home by such methods as I have mentioned, means that the executive has to face the legislature and ministers will lose their office if they forfeit the confidence of the House of Commons. A distinguished American observer has pointed out the concern of that House where the liberties of the subject are involved—for instance, the immediate attack on the Home Secretary if a London policeman has made or is thought to have made a blunder.[13] Over an incident on the night of the 1887 jubilee the Government was defeated. In a debate of a similar kind on another incident in 1928, the Home Secretary says candidly, "I am the servant of the House of Commons; every action I take, every decision I come to in regard to the police can be brought up and discussed here." Forthwith a royal commission was appointed to review the whole subject of police powers and procedure. It reported fully upon the relations of police and public, the obtaining of statements from accused persons, the reliability of police evidence, the possibility of police corruption, and all the rest of it. We sometimes wonder if the principle of ministerial responsibility is as strong as it used to be or as it ought to be. It would be weakened if the civil service abandoned its tradition of anonymity. The development, otherwise helpful, of advisory councils and advisory committees relieves a Minister of some of his anxieties by conciliating opposition in advance, but the use of consultative committees, inside or outside Parliament, reduces responsibility. The committee system is

[13] Felix Frankfurter, summing up the Cincinnati Conference, 1938, *Am. Bar. Jour.*, XXIV (No. 4), 284. See also J. F. Moylan, *Scotland Yard*, "Whitehall series," p. 75.

alternative rather than complementary to ministerial activity as we know it in Britain. It happens to suit the requirements of local government in England. In county councils the chairman with the aid of paid experts in health or education or highways gets through an immense amount of work in committee, and the full meeting of the council registers its approval or, on rare occasions, refers a matter back in order to show its disagreement. In Parliament if a committee controlled the activities of a minister, or if a weak minister were anxious always to shelter himself behind a committee, Britain would lose an indispensable weapon against official oppression and bureaucratic incompetence. The weapon is not a mere unwritten convention; the judges recognize it and even recommend its use. Dicey pointed out in 1915 that the principle of ministerial responsibility had no more solid backing than the prospect that the political majority in the House of Commons, engaged in keeping the Government in office, would censure its own chiefs. This moved Sir Frederick Pollock to remark that all party majorities become minorities sooner or later, and one of the surest ways in which any Government can hasten that process is to acquire a reputation for arbitrary interference with ordinary rights.[14] With the increased interest in Parliamentary affairs and with the new opportunities of assessing the character and abilities of a minister heard on the microphone, it is possible that public opinion in Britain is now more readily mobilized to insist upon Cabinet changes. Although there may seldom be many members

[14] *Law Quarterly Review* (1915), XXXI, 152.

of Parliament who desire a general election, we have seen a change of leadership enforced by democratic methods even during the present war.

A more basic difference between the constitutions of the United States and Britain—if I may be forgiven for mentioning anything so elementary to so learned an audience—is the notorious fact that Britain has no written constitution, no fundamental statute which serves as a touchstone for all other legislation and which cannot be altered save by some specially solemn and dilatory process. In Britain the King in Parliament is all-powerful. There is no Act which cannot be passed and will not be valid within the ordinary limits of judicial interpretation.[15] You know the saying that Parliament can do everything except turn a man into a woman: I believe I could show you a statutory attempt to solve even that biological difficulty. And there is no Act of the British Parliament which cannot be repealed like any other Act. A certain Tudor statute provides that anyone who attempts to secure its repeal shall be guilty of high treason and suffer death and the forfeiture of all his property. I have personal reasons for deprecating publicity for the fact, but repeal of this Act is likely to be proposed by a Statute Law Revision Bill which may some day come before Parliament. Even Magna Carta is not inviolate, though many Englishmen suppose it cannot be touched. Coke, you remember, said that if any statute be made to the contrary

[15] See Sir F. Pollock, *First Book of Jurisprudence*, p. 250, for the story of the survival of the idea that the judges can invalidate an English statute. See also John Dickinson, *Administrative Justice and the Supremacy of Law*, pp. 90–91.

of Magna Carta, it is void. Actually about two-thirds of it has been repealed already. Sentiment will always protect that famous passage which contains the earliest statement of the Rule of Law; but there is no legal obstacle to its repeal—nor, one may add, would British courts give any the less protection to liberty if repeal did take place.

The fact that statutes of the British Parliament cannot be overruled as unconstitutional has its obvious bearing upon the doctrine of the separation of powers. A visitor to the United States is frankly afraid of discussing the value of that doctrine. He has found it emphatically incorporated in the constitutions of various States; he finds it indirectly asserted in the Federal Constitution. An absolute insistence upon the separation of legislative, executive, and judicial power must, he feels, rule out any delegation of legislative power to the executive. He finds definite opinions like that of Mr. Justice Harlan—"that Congress cannot delegate legislative power to the President is a principle universally recognized as vital to the integrity and maintenance of the system of government ordained by the Constitution." [16] Yet he is told that from the earliest years of the United States some such delegation occurred. He reads that "it used to be said that 'Congress may not delegate its powers,' but the rule nowadays has become that Congress may not delegate its powers unless it is convenient to do so." [17] High authority tells him that the Supreme Court of the United States has not

[16] Wichita R. R. & Light Co. v. Public Utilities Comm. of Kansas, 260 U. S. 48.

[17] E. S. Corwin, *The Constitution and What It Means Today* (1st edition), p. 62.

treated the separation of powers as a technical legal doctrine, that the doctrine was not intended to divide the branches into watertight compartments, and that your country has achieved the control of navigation, the regulation of railroad rates, the administration of the Pure Food and Drugs Act, the allocation of wave lengths, and so forth by refusing to be the slave of a sterile dogma.[18] He is given to understand that it was not till 1935, in the *Panama Refining Co. v. Ryan,* that an Act was declared invalid because it failed to separate the powers. He studies that well-known passage in the opinion of Chief Justice Hughes:

> Undoubtedly legislation must often be adapted to complex conditions involving a host of details with which the national legislature cannot deal directly. The Constitution has never been regarded as denying to the Congress the necessary resources of flexibility and practicality which will enable it to perform its function in laying down policies and establishing standards, while leaving to selected instrumentalities the making of subordinate rules within prescribed limits and the determination of facts to which the policy as declared by the legislature is to apply. Without capacity to give authorisations of that sort we should have the anomaly of a legislative power which in many circumstances calling for its exertion would be but a futility.

Goodnow, one of the founders of the school of political science at Columbia University who were mapping out the field of administrative law while it was still *terra incognita* to Britons, suggested that the functions of government were not threefold but twofold—legislative and

[18] F. Frankfurter, *The Public and Its Government,* p. 78.

executive, the judiciary being merely a law-enforcing agency. In the *Rights of Man* Tom Paine had reduced the three-power system to two powers—the legislative, which enacts the laws, and the judiciary, which executes them. Whether the powers be three or two, and, if two, which two, there is no need in Britain to rationalize the doctrine of separation or to "soften it with a quasi." To the English it is a respectable ideal, not even a legal fiction; the multitude of exceptions disproves the rule. There are the fused powers of the Lord Chancellor at the top of the tree and of the magistrates lower down. Those four centralized factory inspectors of 1833 had power to make their own rules, regulations, and orders, to execute the statute with all the powers of a constable, to summon witnesses and adjudicate in proceedings for enforcing penalties with all the powers of a justice, and to send people to prison for not paying fines.[19] In 1806 Lord Ellenborough, Lord Chief Justice of England, accepted a seat in the Cabinet. Political opponents cried out against the unconstitutional fusion of judicial and executive functions and quoted Montesquieu and Blackstone. Government spokesmen blandly replied that precedents were more helpful than theories and that the words of Blackstone, though beautiful, were wild. Precedents were produced, the opposition was beaten, and the doctrine of separation was ignored. Bagehot, you remember, said that the efficient secret of the English constitution was the close

[19] 3 & 4 Will. 4, c. 103. The power to act as magistrates and make rules was soon taken away (7 & 8 Vict. c. 15, s. 2). Compare the fused functions of the Commissioners of Sewers (land drainage authorities) under 23 Hen. 8, c. 5.

union and nearly complete fusion of the executive and legislative powers. In other words by the system of Cabinet government the executive authority is entrusted to a committee consisting of members of the dominant party in the legislature and in the country. The independence of their judges is the aspect most likely to interest the English.

To round off what I want to say on this theme, let me go back to the opinions in *Panama Refining Co. v. Ryan.* The Supreme Court thought—did it not?—that the powers given to the President were legislative and therefore unconstitutional—legislative because they were too general, because, in giving him a discretion, Congress omitted to tell him the policy in the light of which the discretion was to be exercised. Then came the Schechter Poultry case, with a striking opinion by the late Mr. Justice Cardozo. Next year in the Carter Coal case, where the delegation was to an entirely unofficial body, Mr. Justice Sutherland said that a statute which attempts to confer such power undertakes an intolerable and unconstitutional interference with personal liberty and private property. With those last words about liberty and property in your ears, listen to this passage from a British statute enacted last May: [20]

The powers conferred on His Majesty by the Emergency Powers (Defence) Act, 1939 . . . shall . . . include power by Order in Council to make such Defence Regulations making provision for requiring persons to place themselves, their services and their property at the disposal of His

[20] 3 & 4 Geo. 6, c. 20, sometimes popularly referred to as the Everything and Everybody Act.

Majesty as appear to him to be necessary or expedient for securing the public safety, the defence of the Realm, the maintenance of public order or the efficient prosecution of any war in which His Majesty may be engaged, or for maintaining supplies or services essential to the life of the community.

That Act was passed in one afternoon, with no warning, with hardly any copies of the Bill available in advance, and without even the prescribed notice (never, I think, omitted before) that the suspension of the standing orders would be moved. All that anybody said was that the Act ought to have been passed much earlier. The regulations can be challenged in the British courts, but only if they are beyond the powers of that enabling statute, not because they or the enabling Act violate "due process of law" or any constitutional doctrine. They do not need to be "necessary or expedient" for the purposes named; they need only be such as appear to His Majesty to be necessary or expedient. It is the highwater mark of the voluntary surrender of liberty.

The general topic of emergency legislation will be dealt with in my third lecture. Meanwhile let me somehow take a hurried leap forward from the times of Chadwick to the times of today. In Britain the advent of collectivist legislation has been assigned to various dates—1870, 1880, 1906, or other years. By reason of its gradualness it escaped notice. Todd's book on *Parliamentary Government in England,* once a most useful manual, has little to say of departmental activities in its original edition in 1866. The second edition, in 1887, has a separate chapter on "Legislation by Public Departments." It recalls how the judges protested in 1871 when a High Court of Justice Bill proposed to authorize a committee of the Privy Council to make or alter rules of procedure. The judges would probably have been allowed their own way by the Privy Council in the making of the rules, but they took the constitutional point that the judicature should be independent of the executive. Let Parliament fix the guiding principles, they said, and let the judges settle the subordinate points of procedure.

The judges got their way and regained a power of prescribing rules about procedure which perhaps they always inherently possessed. This little storm over delegated legislation in the eighteen-seventies was soon back in its tea-cup. The judges, you see, did not mind so long as the delegation was in the right hands. There was occasional protest over the exercises of the departmental power to vary schemes under the Endowed Schools Acts; tampering with ancient charities is apt to be controversial.[21] Otherwise the Victorian age was not much excited over departmental encroachments in England when once the Chadwick period was over. The new laws were not lawyers' laws; lawyers did not study them. Supervigilant sentries might have noticed suspicious signs across the front line, but a trusted watchman chanted reassuringly that all was well. This was Albert Venn Dicey, whose attractive Oxford lectures on the *Law of the Constitution* explained to generations of insular Englishmen the com-

[21] For the successful moving of a hostile address under 32 & 33 Vict. c. 56, s. 41, see Hansard, CCVII, 862–902, 962.

forting superiority of their system. On one of his visits to America Dicey confessed that the English had a habit of identifying their own successes with the decrees of Providence, though he was bold enough to hint to his hosts that the same might perhaps be said of other English-speaking peoples. Dicey was a stylist; in Bentham's handsome words about Blackstone, he taught jurisprudence to speak the language of the scholar and the gentleman. All the young men who studied Dicey for their bar examinations read him with avidity; in later life, as barristers or judges or leader writers, they never forgot him. He expounded the Rule of Law which he found to be a feature both of the United States and of Britain, though far more fully developed, he thought, in the United States. To Dicey the two chief elements of that rule were these. First, that no man should be punishable or should be made to suffer in body or goods except for a distinct breach of law established in the ordinary legal manner before the ordinary courts: in other words, the absence of arbitrary power or even wide discretionary power on the part of the government. Secondly, equality before the law, the amenability of everybody, high or low, to the ordinary law of the land and to the jurisdiction of the ordinary tribunals without any exemption for officials.

It was in this latter context that Dicey gave an unlucky twist to the words "administrative law" in England which has scarcely yet been straightened out. Those words are the obvious translation of the *droit administratif* to which he so copiously refers. He wasted pity on the French for being at the mercy of officials whom they could not bring into the ordinary courts, when in truth the special courts for deciding disputes between citizens and officials in France were working most acceptably and giving a practical remedy where English citizens got none. He thought that the France of his day was suffering from the *sequelae* of the same monarchical despotism that had afflicted England when the Tudors and Stuarts strained the use of the prerogative. To him departmental discretion was arbitrary discretion. He thought of officials mainly as potential oppressors—which was ungrateful, because he was for fourteen years junior counsel to the Inland Revenue, a department which not everybody would regard as benevolent. He over-estimated the value of an Englishman's right to sue any official personally; he under-estimated the procedural difficulties of suing the Crown, the effect of the immunity of the Crown in tort, and the non-application to a government department of the rule that a master is responsible for the actions of his servants. If the driver of a mail-van negligently runs over me in England, I know from Dicey that I can sue the driver. But it is the Post Office—in loose language the public purse—out of which I want to extract the substantial damages which I hope to be awarded. Actually the system does not work too badly. The Government lawyers will probably undertake the defence of the Government servant, and the Treasury will probably pay the damages. But that is an act of grace, a concession which could be refused. The King, who can do no wrong, is not easily dragged into his own courts as defendant. If the Postmaster-General happened himself to be driving the mail-van, I know from

Dicey that I could sue him personally and that he could not escape by saying that he was driving on urgent Government business or that his action was an act of State. That is not the complete safeguard, but it is something; it represents, in Maitland's words, "a great deal of what we mean when we talk of English liberty."

In tending to limit "administrative law" to a supposedly continental system of delinquent officials escaping from the jurisdiction of the ordinary courts, Dicey set up his own nine-pins and knocked them happily over. He said very little about the general problem of the privileged position of the Crown as litigant, though he lived to have first-hand acquaintance with it, for his last appearance in the courts as a practising barrister was to hold a brief for the Government in the Shoreham aerodrome case, where the prerogative was vigorously asserted.[22] The official legal advisers of the Crown, like the judges, became well aware of this general problem in the last war and the years that followed. In 1921 Lord Chancellor Birkenhead appointed the Attorney-General, Sir Gordon Hewart, afterwards Lord Hewart, as chairman of a strong committee to consider proposals that the position of the Crown as litigant should be assimilated to that of other litigants and that the Crown should be liable to be sued for its servants' negligence. Prompt action might have done much to clip the claws of Whitehall, but the chance was lost. The committee took six years to report. It then

[22] *In re* a Petition of Right [1915] 3 K. B. 649. The locality of the aerodrome was not named for military reasons. The case went to the House of Lords, but no judgment was given, the Crown making payment.

produced an admirable and well-drafted Bill, which, except for a few clauses which found their way into law in other contexts, has remained in its pigeon-hole ever since. There were no votes in it; there was an element of theory, and, as all Englishmen know, once one embarks upon theory, one does not know where one will find oneself. The advisers of the Crown may have feared that, if the Crown were defendant, juries would award huge sums in damages as they tend to do against supposedly wealthy railway or insurance companies. Whatever the reasons, this remedy against departments is still withheld, though there has been a notable simplification of procedure in granting the prerogative writs of certiorari, mandamus, and prohibition.

Meanwhile departmental activity, much increased in the last war, had thrust itself upon the public attention. Tolerated while the guns were still firing, it outstayed its welcome, as abnormal departmental activity so often does. Looking around and taking stock in the subsequent period of reconstruction, the country suddenly noticed a vast mass of delegated legislation, a multitude of non-judicial tribunals. The bench and the bar suspected a sinister attempt to exclude common-law jurisdiction. Dicey had told the islanders that so far as administrative law was concerned they could sleep peacefully in their beds, and now all the alarm bells were ringing. One brilliantly written attack upon this "new despotism" accused the civil service of conspiring to destroy the independence of the judiciary. Forthwith another authoritative committee of investigation was set up by the Lord Chancellor. It was a well-balanced body. There were six members of the House of Commons; there were five practising lawyers (one of them, Sir Leslie Scott, now Lord Justice Scott, had special knowledge of Crown proceedings, because he had been Solicitor General); there were three civil servants with wide and ripe experience of administration. The inclusion of Professor Holdsworth ensured the accuracy of the historical background, that of Professor Laski ensured acute criticism of ideas too complacently held. The Committee on Ministers' Powers (sometimes called the Donoughmore Committee after its first chairman) was formally invited to consider the powers exercised by departments by way of delegated legislation or of judicial or quasi-judicial decision and to report what safeguards were desirable or necessary to secure the constitutional principles of the sovereignty of Parliament and the supremacy of the law. In other words the questions were whether Britain had gone off the Dicey standard and, if so, what was the quickest way back.

To the detailed findings of this inquest, published in 1932, I hope to refer later. The broad result was reassuring. In England, as perhaps also in America, things were evidently not yet so bad as the critics feared. The "new despotism" of Whitehall, having thus been put upon its trial, was, in Lord Eustace Percy's phrase, dismissed with a farthing fine. The report of the Lord Chancellor's committee showed signs of the usual element of compromise —the price paid for unanimity. There is a statement on one page that the outspoken, even if exaggerated, criticism or attacks which had led up to the investigation had performed a useful service.[23] There is another that there was no foundation for the suggestion that civil servants had attempted or desired to secure arbitrary power for themselves or for their departments.[24] Concerning the delegation of legislative power, the committee concluded that the system was "both legitimate and constitutionally desirable for certain purposes, within certain limits and under certain safeguards." It was "indispensable" and "inevitable." [25] As for the existing practice of Parliament in permitting the exercise of judicial and quasi-judicial powers by ministers and of judicial powers by ministerial tribunals, there was "nothing radically wrong" about it, "subject of course to proper safeguards against abuse." The result must have been reasonably good, because the report failed to satisfy the extreme critics on both flanks. The right wing thought it too soporific; these were the warriors whose plan of campaign proposed to wipe out all delegated legislation and all administrative tribunals rather than to prescribe the limits of tolerance. On the other hand, the more progressive commentators had been disappointed that the devotion to Dicey's memory dominated the terms of reference. It is perhaps a small matter that his principle of equality before the law is hard to reconcile with the privileged position conceded to judges and sometimes also to policemen.[26] What is more serious, they say, is that his Rule of Law assumes that the purpose of the constitution is to

[23] Report of Committee on Ministers' Powers (1932), Cmd. 4060, p. 7.
[24] *Ibid.*, pp. 7, 59.
[25] *Ibid.*, pp. 51, 53, 58.
[26] J. H. Morgan, Introduction to Gleeson Robinson's *Public Authorities and Legal Liability*, pp. xlix–liv.

protect individual rights,[27] whereas the purpose of large groups of statutes (at any rate in Britain) is to attack them. Some might answer that this is an over-simplified statement which confuses purpose with effect. The supremacy of the law is surely a matter of protecting individual rights. One eminent writer has challengingly stated that the whole purpose of our English Housing Acts is to remedy social evils by interfering with the rights of landowners.[28] If the sponsors of those Acts had proclaimed that to be their object, does anyone imagine that the Acts would have been so easily passed? The difference indicates a healthy clash between political philosophies. If the progressives seek to write off Dicey as a poor old Victorian Whig who could not escape from the background of his individualistic dogmatism, his ghost might legitimately rejoin that the ideologies of his opponents are unmistakable too. The critics describe Dicey's Rule of Law as either a myth or a platitude. His conclusions must be wrong, they say, because he started by misinforming himself about *droit administratif;* they are irrelevant because he assumed that the legal system to be regulated is the legal system of *laissez faire*.[29] If so, the inquest held by the Committee on Ministers' Powers was misconceived, and a great chance was lost to work out a new and logical theory of administrative law in sympathy with modern ten-

27 See E. C. S. Wade, Preface to 9th ed. of Dicey, *Law of the Constitution*, p. xii.

28 W. I. Jennings, "Courts and Administrative Law—The Experience of English Housing Legislation," *Harvard Law Review* (1936), XLIX, 451.

29 *Ibid.*, p. 430. In citing these views of Mr. Jennings, I wish to remind readers of his generous and graceful tribute "In Praise of Dicey," in *Public Administration* (1935), XIII, 123.

dencies, and a new and standardized set of co-ordinated administrative tribunals such as Mr. W. A. Robson has outlined in his *Justice and Administrative Law.*

The findings of the Committee on Ministers' Powers are not the framing of a constitution. They are merely a guide which the legislator and the draftsman can, but need not, follow. Their authority is derived from the reputation and experience of the members of the committee and the obvious care with which a large body of evidence was gathered and studied. Tacitly accepted by an unexcited country, they entrench the tradition of affectionate solicitude for the ancient landmarks which Dicey so lovingly tended—Magna Carta and the Bill of Rights and the victories for personal liberty and freedom of discussion. The disappointed critics must just continue their task of educating the electorate and not, like enlightened but impatient Chadwicks, complain of the opposition of "sinister interests" and dash on too far ahead of public opinion. The committee's report met the fate of that earlier Lord Chancellor's Committee on Crown Proceedings. A few minor recommendations found their way to the statute-book; [30] major matters are held over, and at present there are more pressing concerns. Yet there were unobtrusive gains. The civil service was shaken up. Departments were called upon to justify themselves. Officials and non-officials learnt one another's points of view in a frank and friendly cross-examination of witnesses, whose published testimony is a mine of information for anyone who might wish to study the working of insular democ-

30 See Appendix, p. 175, below.

racy. Not the least revealing part will be the adroit questions put by the three distinguished civil servants who were members of the committee and who knew the answers already.

Bolingbroke, the wayward author of *The Patriot King*, somewhere cites with approval the dictum of Machiavelli that

> of all governments those are the best which, by the natural effect of their original constitutions are frequently renewed or drawn back to their first principles . . . No government can be of long duration where this does not happen from time to time.

These words come aptly to the mind when one reads certain great opinions of the Supreme Court at Washington. Somewhat in the same reverent spirit, yet with a like determination not to be blind to social progress, the Committee on Ministers' Powers drew back the islanders to the Dicey tradition in a period of reaction from the stimulus which a world-wide war had given to the executive. Already the pendulum has swung back once more, and the executive in Britain needs to be armed with even greater powers in an even greater crisis. The voice of abstract theory, never very strong, is temporarily dominated by the strident demands of national efficiency for the achievement of a single aim. Democracies cannot tie their own hands if they are fighting for self-preservation.

2. Delegated Legislation

A numerous assembly is as little fitted for the direct business of legislation as for that of administration.
—JOHN STUART MILL, REPRESENTATIVE GOVERNMENT (1861)

THE ASPECT of administrative law which my first lecture tried to present to you was the faded vision of the outburst of centralization and officialdom in Britain in the eighteen-thirties. Then we skipped a century and found the nineteen-thirties re-discovering the excessive activities of governmental agencies. We glanced at the report of the Lord Chancellor's Committee on Ministers' Powers in 1932—an investigation which has had recent parallels in the United States. One of the two subjects which the committee was invited to examine was the delegation (some people might call it the surrender) of legislative power by the British Parliament to Government departments. That rather technical and forbidding subject is the aspect which I offer you today.

Dicey, the late-Victorian prophet, had blessed rather than cursed such delegation. More liberally minded than some of his disciples, he thought the practice would give us better laws and would leave legislators more liberty to concentrate on big principles. That was the plan deliberately adopted in France, and for once Dicey found something French to admire.

Medieval controversialists used to drive home their

points with a text from the Bible. Political philosophers fortify themselves with a few words from Plato and Aristotle. Both oracles discussed the difficulty of adjusting a general statement of law to particular cases. Plato played with the fancy that the best possible government would be a perfectly wise ruler unfettered by any laws whatever; [1] conversely the worst possible would be an unwise ruler enjoying the same freedom. You remember the classic passage— What with the differences between one man and another and one set of facts and another and the fluidity of human affairs, no skill could promulgate a simple rule for all persons and all time. Yet that, says Plato, is just what the law tries to do, like some self-sufficient ignorant fellow who won't let anyone act contrary to his orders or even ask a question, not even if something turns up which is an improvement on those orders. Aristotle follows suit.[2] All law is universal, but there are some things about which one simply cannot make a statement which will be correct. In those cases the law must deal with the majority, though well aware of the risk of error. The error is neither in the law nor in the legislator but in the nature of the thing. If the legislator errs through over-simplification, it will be right to correct any omission by a special decree. When that plan of special treatment was applied in Anglo-Saxon history, our experience was unlucky. The Bill of Rights had to check it by declaring illegal the pretended power of suspending laws or dispensing with the execution of laws. And yet some kind of dispensing power is

1 *Politicus*, 294.

2 *Nicomachean Ethics*, V, x, 4 (1137B).

inevitable; it is common enough today in British statutes about factories or patents or merchant shipping. After all, the favourite approach of legislatures to many modern problems is to adopt some plan of statutory registration and licensing, whether it is for ships, aircraft or motor cars, or for medical practice, sale of narcotic drugs or intoxicating liquors, vivisection of animals or what else. The licensing system is close enough to the dispensing system. Its value and success depend on the public confidence felt in the licensing body. Prerogative licensing, as seen in the days of Elizabeth and James I, threatened the country with favouritism and corruption. Statutory licensing ought to mean that the country thinks it has found someone to trust. That is the difference. It would be a pity if we allowed our inherited suspicions of the earlier method to survive against the later.

In considering the relation of permanent statute law to periodical minor adjustments Plato has this apt passage:

> In all matters involving a mass of petty detail the law-giver must leave gaps; rules and up-to-date amendments must be made from year to year by persons who have constant experience from year to year in these things and who are taught by practice until a satisfactory code is finally agreed upon to regulate such proceedings.[3]

Almost the very words of Plato seem to be echoed in this official minute on delegated legislation written in 1893 by Sir Henry Jenkyns, second in the line of Parliamentary Counsel in Britain:[4]

[3] *Laws*, VI, 772B; *cf.* 769D.
[4] He succeeded Lord Thring and preceded Sir Courtenay Ilbert.

Statutory rules are in themselves of great public advantage because the details which are the subject of them can thus be regulated after a Bill passes into an Act with greater care and minuteness, and with better adaptation to local or other special circumstances, than they possibly can be in the passage of a Bill through Parliament. Besides they mitigate the inelasticity which would often otherwise make an Act unworkable, and are susceptible of modifications from time to time by the government department at any time of the year as circumstances arise.

Among the primary justifications of the delegation of the legislative power, then, is what Chief Justice Hughes called flexibility and practicality. Now flexibility is a word of flexible meaning. To anyone who like myself has official duties which give him a superficial rather than an intelligent outlook on legislative results—not a bird's-eye so much as a worm's-eye view, an indexer's interest, rather quantitative than qualitative—who sees so many ranges of statute law as tumble-down ill-built houses crying out for demolition or orderly reconstruction, who knows that the cry is unheard because the legislature and the departments are busy elsewhere, who realizes that the tempo and the choice of legislation are dictated by the Cabinet, behind whom are the party whips, behind whom again is some anonymous figure (not the least important in the British constitution) with a time-table and a stop-watch, saying, "You have so many discussion-hours between now and the end of the session: you can get such and such Bills through in that time but not this Bill or that Bill, and, if you concede a day to a full-dress debate on this or that subject, you must jettison such and such items on this list"—to anyone who sees that aspect of law-making, "flexibility" means, first and foremost, legislative speed. The commonest official excuse in side-tracking some proposal is "This would require legislation for which no Parliamentary time is available." Statutes must be avoided if possible; instead, for instance, of passing an *ad hoc* Census Act every ten years, we substitute a permanent Census Act capable of being applied by Order in Council whenever wanted.[5] Statutes must, as Dicey thought, confine themselves to outlines and principles. It must, as Chief Justice Marshall said as long ago as 1825, be left to those who are to act under the general statutory provisions to "fill up the details."[6] Legislators must not be too jealous to hand technical matters over to experts. No one can deny that there are experts of all kinds in every legislature, and no one should suggest that we do wisely to hand over all law-making to experts—indeed the fate of Chadwick points a moral there. But there is a reservoir of accumulated knowledge and experience outside the legislature which it is a pity not to use. We can trust a committee of judges and legal practitioners to make rules of court. We can trust some recognized organization with proper academic and professional qualifications to say what is a dangerous poison or what is a safety lamp proper for coal miners to use. We ought to be able to trust expert administrators, if the country in the persons of its elected representatives can in the long run control them through some vulnerable ministerial

[5] 10 & 11 Geo. 5, c. 41.
[6] Wayman v. Southard, 10 Wheat. at pp. 42–43.

head or otherwise and if the Chadwicks do not get out of hand, to work out a policy which the legislature has adopted and prescribed. The question is one of confidence (as I said just now) and of competence and convenience. Chadwick himself put these aspects of legislative speed and specialized technique into one of his bluebooks.[7] The new poor-law regulations, he said, would have to be numerous; they must be uniform, but they must be varied periodically. Unless Parliament was to do nothing but occupy itself with discussions on details of workhouse management, it would be impossible to make any great change.

> A great many regulations, however ably devised, must be experimental. Here unforeseen and apparently unimportant details might baffle the best plans if there were not the means of making immediate alteration. Suppose a general regulation were prescribed by Act of Parliament and it was found to want alteration; you must wait a whole year or more for an Act of Parliament to amend it, or the law must be broken. A central authority might make the alteration or supply unforeseen omissions in a day or two.

If it were a question of workhouse diet, it could take medical opinion promptly. Who would ever think of applying to Parliament to say whether four or five ounces of butter was a proper ration in particular cases, or whether the butter should be Dutch or Irish, or whether the old women's under-petticoats should be flannel or baize and how wide or how long? Those details, said

[7] Appendix A to the Poor Law Commissioners' Report (cited by the Webbs, in *English Local Government, English Poor Law History*, Part II, p. 79).

Chadwick, would be beneath the dignity of grave legislators; yet, as he insisted in his bureaucratic way, on such details good or bad management would depend.

Perhaps an Englishman might assume that the three chief justifications for delegated legislation are the same in the United States as in Britain—first, the limits of the time of the legislature; secondly, the limits of the aptitude of the legislature (not merely its lack of competence in technical fields but also its sheer inability to act at all in many situations where direction is wanted); and thirdly, the need of some weapon for coping with situations created by emergency (whether it be a cholera epidemic or a general strike or a total war) or situations arising when the legislature is not sitting. The American Bar seems ready to give delegated legislation a welcome after a searching inquiry. In England our General Council of the Bar is too conservatively and exclusively concerned with professional interests to indulge in any such speculative investigation; but, as we saw last week, the Committee on Ministers' Powers (of which several barristers were members and before which the chairman of the Bar Council gave interesting evidence) concluded that delegation was inevitable and indispensable. The committee could hardly have decided otherwise when the two first witnesses, public servants speaking with special experience and responsibility, testified that it would be impossible to produce the amount and the kind of legislation which Parliament desired to pass and which the people of Britain were supposed to want if it should become necessary to insert in the statutes themselves any considerable part of what is now left to delegated legislation.

If members of the British public ever thought about delegation, there is no reason to suppose that their view would be hostile. Corporate and municipal bodies have been making by-laws from time immemorial. Popular opinion is ready to respect laws made by any well-known authority. Is it too trivial to look for an analogy in the regulation of the country's peace-time diversions—the cricket, which is a national game in England; the golf, which is an imported counter-irritant; and the card-playing, which, as Dr. Johnson said, generates kindness and consolidates society? The English have accepted the rules, without which these pastimes cannot be enjoyed, from the Marylebone Cricket Club at Lord's, the Royal and Ancient Society at St. Andrews, and the Portland Club in London. They do not know the actual legislators by sight or by name, but they have been content with their laws.

The Committee on Ministers' Powers qualified its tolerance of delegated legislation by specifying four exceptional types which would require special vigilance. May I say a few words on these? They seem so inevitable and indispensable that one may expect to detect them on both sides of the Atlantic.

As the first of the four the committee named the power to legislate on matters of principle or even to impose taxation.[8] In theory, of course, the legislature ought to

[8] Another type of exceptional delegation mentioned by the committee (delegation conferring so wide a discretion that it is impossible to know

settle the principles and delegate the details, but occasionally the legislature shirks its duty. In 1925 a big consolidation of Acts relating to the Supreme Court in England was waiting upon the passing of a preliminary amending Bill. This amending Bill was delayed by inability to settle the question how far juries should be dispensed with in civil trials. Previous war-time restrictions on jury trials were ripe for replacement by permanent law. Now there could be few more vital matters of principle than the right to a jury; yet, to get the difficulty out of the way, it was arranged that this issue should be left to be governed by rules of court.[9] Principle, in fact, is dealt with as procedure; we need no reminder of the importance of procedure in the protection of rights. Later, in 1931, there was some general misgiving over abuses of State relief for unemployment. To remove the discussion from the political atmosphere of the House of Commons, it was enacted that these scandals (euphemistically called "anomalies") should be dealt with by departmental regulations.[10] Turning to the United States, one finds Mr. James Hart, whose work I often find myself quoting, remarking that it may sometimes be politically inexpedient for Congress to define a clear-cut policy. When the Labor Relations Act was passed, he

---

what limit the legislature intended to impose) is so close to the delegation of power to legislate on matters of principle that I have not dealt with it separately. The committee cited the same instance for the two types, namely, the vague power given to Chadwick's Poor Law Board in 1834 to make rules generally "for the management of the poor."

[9] See 15 & 16 Geo. 5, c. 28, s. 3, superseded by 15 & 16 Geo. 5, c. 49, s. 99(1)(*h*).

[10] See 21 & 22 Geo. 5, c. 36; see also 24 & 25 Geo. 5, c. 29, s. 11(2) (orders).

says, a split was becoming visible on the issue of craft versus industrial unions. "Congress left to the Board the task of selecting the appropriate bargaining unit in each case as it arose. To do more would have been impracticable at a time when the issue was still an open one." [11]

As for the delegation of power to tax, although historically there is no legislative function more jealously claimed by the legislature, it is hard to see how a tariff system can be operated without delegation. In England, under the Import Duties Act of 1932 and other statutes, the House of Commons surrendered to the Treasury the power to impose *ad valorem* duties and to alter the free list. The Treasury was to act on the suggestions of an independent advisory committee; some degree of House of Commons control was retained by enacting that the Treasury orders would lapse after twenty-eight days unless earlier confirmed by a resolution of the House. In the United States the Tariff Act of 1890 authorized Congress to fix duties whenever the President found the other country's duties to be reciprocally unequal and unreasonable. This function of the President was declared to be mere fact finding, not legislative "in any real sense"; he did not make a law, but merely declared the event upon which the expressed will of the legislature would take effect.[12] It was different when more flexible tariff arrangements empowered the President to fix the duty above or below the statutory limit, subject to investigation and report by the Tariff Commission. Did not the

[11] *Exercise of Rule-Making Power,* &c. (President's Committee on Administrative Management), p. 15.

[12] Field v. Clark (1892), 143 U. S. 649.

late Mr. Justice Cardozo confess in the Norwegian Nitrogen case that what was done by the Tariff Commission and the President in changing tariff rates to suit new conditions was "in substance a delegation, though a permissible one, of the legislative power"? [13]

Another exceptional type of delegation, in the eyes of the Committee on Ministers' Powers, was the authority to alter statutes. The very idea that subordinate legislation should ever be allowed to tamper with the sacred text of a statute is at first sight shocking. Why, ask the legislators, do we sit here and debate so carefully the exact language of the prospective law if someone outside can presently alter it by a stroke of the pen? Why, ask the citizens, do we vote to send our representatives to the legislature if some non-elected official can undo their handiwork?

In England the practice is neither recent nor rare.[14] It takes various forms. There is the power to extend a statutory category.[15] There is the class of provision where Parliament inserts some specific details, but, realizing that they may require periodical adjustment, does not hesitate to delegate the power to alter. Thus when English legal procedure was reformed in 1873 by the fusion of law and equity, the statute contained a tentative code

13 Norwegian Nitrogen Products Co. v. U. S. (1933) 288 U. S. 305.

14 See 6 Ric. 2, Stat. 1, c. 5, and 11 Ric. 2, c. 11, for a power for the Chancellor to vary a statute which was found prejudicial and grievous. Compare 2 & 3 Will. 4, c. 60.

15 See 39 & 40 Geo. III. c. 80, s. 9 (quarantine for plague, or diseases declared by proclamation to be of the nature of plague), and 45 & 46 Vict. c. 73, s. 10 (ancient monuments). Compare the power to compile a category in 3 & 4 Geo. 5, c. 32, s. 6 (ancient monuments).

of procedure but delegated a power to alter or vary the code. Two years later an amending Act enabled rules of court to modify any provisions in any previous statute dealing with the practice and procedure of the courts concerned.[16] Is there not a significant American parallel in the statute passed by Congress in 1934 to give the Supreme Court of the United States authority to make and publish rules? The rules were to take effect six months after their promulgation, "and thereafter all laws in conflict therewith shall be of no force or effect." [17]

Another kind of intervention by order upon statute is the press-the-button procedure which appoints a date for the statute to operate. In Britain, in the rush of modern law-making, many laws tumble out of the oven half baked. Either the country is not yet ready for them or administrative preparations have yet to be made. The working of the new laws will often depend on the setting up of some new organization or on the framing of regulations. It is not possible to begin drafting the regulations till the final form of the enabling legislation is fixed. The statute may not be passed till the eve of the holidays, when it may be difficult to consult interests affected. Parliament therefore enables the department concerned to appoint the day when the statute shall operate. "This is to be the law," it says; "carry on when you are ready." The alternative is to fix a definite future date in the statute itself; but, where this has been done, it will need an amending Act if it turns out that further postpone-

[16] 36 & 37 Vict. c. 66, ss. 69, 74; 38 & 39 Vict. c. 77, s. 24.

[17] 48 Stat. 1064. See also the Overman Act of 1918 (40 Stat. 556), and the Reorganization Act of 1939 (53 Stat. 561).

ment is wanted.[18] Pressing the button for a statute to take effect will sometimes mean that other enactments will simultaneously cease to have effect. There are English instances of power to terminate Acts by orders both directly and indirectly,[19] as well as to continue enactments by order.[20] May I mention King George III? He was authorized in the significant year of 1778 to appoint commissioners for treating with Americans for the redress of grievances and to empower the commissioners to suspend a certain prohibitory Act which was attempting to strangle trade upon your eastern seaboard. A few years later he was given power to repeal or to suspend any statutes relating to the American colonies in order to remove impediments to the conclusion of a peace.[21] As in the case of machinery for operating a tariff, the legislature provides the gun and prescribes the target, but leaves to the executive the task of pressing the trigger. Cases like *Field v. Clark* and *the Brig Aurora* seem to show that the value of this legislative device is appreciated in the United States. There are plenty of instances of what Mr. J. P. Comer once called "contingent legislation." In Britain it has been invaluable in securing imperial or

[18] See 37 & 38 Vict. c. 83 (changes in English legal procedure) and 15 & 16 Geo. 5, c. 4 (changes in the law of property).

[19] 11 & 12 Geo. 5, c. 64, s. 3(4), and the Spanish crisis measures (1 Edw. 8 & 1 Geo. 6, c. 1, s. 2(5) and c. 19, s. 4(6)). The emergency legislation of the last war came to an end on the date declared by Order in Council to be the termination of the war (8 & 9 Geo. 5, c. 59); the emergency legislation of the present war will expire on the date declared by Order in Council to be the end of the emergency (2 & 3 Geo. 6, c. 67, s. 7(3)).

[20] 29 & 30 Vict. c. 2, s. 11 (cattle disease).

[21] 18 Geo. 3, c. 13, ss. 4, 5; 22 Geo. 3, c. 46 (temporary). For an earlier example of the device in foreign politics, see 25 Hen. 8, c. 21, s. 29.

international reciprocity. Statutes create machinery for reciprocal enforcement of judgments, reciprocal recognition of professional qualifications, or reciprocal relief from double income tax. As soon as an oversea country makes what is deemed reasonably equivalent provision, mutuality can be arranged; if reciprocity fails, the arrangement can be cancelled.

Of all the types of orders which alter statutes, the so-called "Henry VIII clause," sometimes inserted in big and complicated Acts, has probably caused the greatest flutter in England. It enables the Minister by order to modify the Act itself so far as necessary for bringing it into operation. Anyone who will look to see what sort of orders have been made under this power will find them surprisingly innocuous.[22] The device is partly a draftsman's insurance policy, in case he has overlooked something, and is partly due to the immense body of local Acts in England creating special difficulties in particular areas. These local Acts are very hard to trace, and the draftsman could never be confident that he has examined them all in advance. The Henry VIII clause ought, of course, to be effective for a short time only.

Orders which tamper with the text of statutes are usually innocent enough. Often they are purely consequential; if the draftsman had time to work out all the textual changes required by some amendment of the law, no doubt he would be delighted to effect them by direct authority of a statute. Draftsmen, however, have to

[22] See John Willis, *Parliamentary Powers of English Government Departments* (1933), p. 152.

shun delights and live laborious days, and anyhow the opportunities of amendment must be gathered, like rosebuds, while they may. In 1920 the British Parliament granted a large measure of autonomy to Northern Ireland in a controversial atmosphere. Existing statutory references to Ireland as a whole had to be converted into references to Northern Ireland, the new governmental unit. Any mention of the Supreme Court of Ireland would have to mean the Supreme Court of Northern Ireland, the *Dublin Gazette* would become the *Belfast Gazette,* and so forth. Power was given to adapt previous Acts for this purpose by Order in Council. One highly expert draftsman worked at nothing else for many months; orders were still being made for a year or two after the Act was passed, and points of difficulty are appearing twenty years later.[23] The same device was needed in the Government of India Act, 1935. Previously Burma had been administered as part of India. In the previous Acts India included Burma. The 1935 Act made Burma independent of India, as well as converting Aden into a separate colony. The result was that all over the statute-book wherever there was a previous reference to India it was necessary to adapt it by adding the words "or Burma" or "and Burma" or otherwise and perhaps also to insert words about Aden. The consequential Order in Council, authorized for this object, altered the text of over fifty statutes, and that was not the end of it.[24] Had this legisla-

[23] See 10 & 11 Geo. 5, c. 67, ss. 69, 70, and entries in *Index to Statutory Powers and Rules and Orders in Force* (1939), p. 734.

[24] See 26 Geo. 5 & 1 Edw. 8, c. 2, s. 311(5), and S. R. & O. 1937 (No. 230) p. 963.

tion for Northern Ireland and India had to wait till all these consequential adjustments could be worked out and incorporated in the original Bills themselves, the time-table would have been upset and the political tide might have been missed.

The process of adapting Acts by orders is not quite so straightforward where the adaptation occurs in referential legislation. In 1929 a Bill proposed to carry out the policy of having fewer and bigger local authorities in Scotland. It provided for abolishing parish councils which were small-scale units. During debate on the Bill it was rather suddenly decided to create a new kind of medium-size body, namely, the district council. Clauses for this purpose were inserted, but there was no time to work out details such as the arrangements for electing the new district councillors; the Bill therefore applied to district councillors the statutory provisions relating to the election of county councillors in rural areas "subject to such modifications and adaptations as the Secretary of State may by order prescribe." [25]

This is an awkward way to legislate, but it is at any rate preferable to get a definite text, by whatever means achieved, than to rely on words of general application and to leave us guessing which enactments are applied and how far.

It is usual in Britain to insist that if an order alters a statute, the order shall require confirmation by a resolution of both Houses of Parliament. This means, of course, that anyone who wants to note up in his statutes these

[25] 19 & 20 Geo. 5, c. 25, s. 25(4); see also S. R. & O. 1932 (No. 825) p. 406.

textual alterations made by orders has to watch not only for the order but also for the Parliamentary confirmation of it.

From this long digression may I return to discuss one last type of delegation which the Committee on Ministers' Powers described as exceptional? It is that which purports to put the subordinate legislation beyond the reach of attack in the law-courts. The difference between direct and subordinate legislation in Britain is that the direct legislation (the statute) cannot be challenged in the courts, whereas the subordinate legislation (the rule or regulation or order made under the statute) can. If, therefore, the statute contains some such formula as that the rules, regulations, or orders made under it "shall have effect as if enacted in this Act," the result is that the subordinate legislation is no more challengeable than the statute itself. So, at least, we always thought in England on the authority of a decision of the House of Lords given in 1894, where Lord Herschell seemed unable to find any other meaning in the words.[26] The words indeed meant little; if the rules were *intra vires,* they must anyhow have just as much force as the provisions of the enabling Act itself. When Sir Courtenay Ilbert published his book on *Legislative Methods and Forms* in 1901, he warned draftsmen that the formula "shall have effect as if enacted in this Act" should not as a rule be put into a Bill. He thought the words were merely declaratory.[27]

[26] Institute of Patent Agents v. Lockwood [1894] A. C. 347.

[27] The formula has occurred in English statutes, where it was desired to secure statutory effect for a non-statutory document, as in 37 Hen. 8, c. 12 (award of the Archbishop of Canterbury concerning London

Judicial ingenuity need no longer be expended in explaining away the decision of 1894, since the House of Lords has now declared in the Yaffé case that the insertion of the formula does not prevent the courts from pronouncing upon the validity of the delegated legislation.[28] The Committee on Ministers' Powers, while conspicuously anxious to preserve judicial supervision, considered that in exceptional cases challenge was undesirable—for instance, cases of town-planning orders under which property changes hands or "stock regulations" under which a local authority or public undertaking borrows money. There must be finality in such cases. The legitimate interests of property, finance, and business may reasonably demand certainty of the law. Mr. James Hart has emphasized the insecurity of those interests if, in the governmental regulation of business, administrative action should subsequently be held by the courts to have been incorrect and invalid. He draws attention to the amendments of the Securities Act of 1933 and the Securities Exchange Act of 1934. Congress there expressly enacted that no provision of these statutes imposing any liability should apply to any act done or omitted in good faith in conformity with regulations, notwithstanding that such regulations might thereafter be held invalid

---

tithes), or to link a schedule to an Act, as in 53 Geo. 3, c. 123, s. 44, at a time when schedules were unfamiliar as a drafting device. It may have been applied to rules and orders analogously. The validity of rules and orders was in doubt at first: see 11 & 12 Vict. c. 107, s. 4 (diseases of animals) and 29 & 30 Vict. c. 15. See *Minutes of Evidence* before the Committee on Ministers' Powers, p. 41 (answer 517).

[28] [1931] A. C. 494.

for any reason by judicial or other authority. He hopes to see this assurance extended in connexion with other regulatory legislation.[29]

Having now exhausted what in Britain are regarded as exceptional types of delegation, requiring special vigilance, may I say something of possible safeguards? Professor Lindsay Rogers, in his kind words of introduction to today's lecture, recalled that I last lectured on delegated legislation in 1921. Search for a fresh foothold on demobilization after the last war—if you will forgive the egotism of these autobiographical reminiscences—happened to have ended in an apprenticeship in the office of the Editor of Statutory Rules and Orders in London. This official has, among other duties, the responsibility for registering the delegated legislation, giving each rule and order a serial number, and supervising its formal publication. My previous acquaintance with this field of law-making was as distant as that of other common-law practitioners. The lectures upon it which I delivered by the tolerance of the law school at Cambridge in England, with all the confidence of comparative youth and with all the ignorance which a bare eighteen-month experience had not dispelled, ventured to put forward five safeguards for the public in the making of rules and orders. May I review them in the light of riper acquaintance? I had been pointing out that the primary check is political supervision and pressure. The simple remedy for the abuse of delegation is the repeal of the delegating statute.

[29] *Exercise of Rule-making Power,* &c. (President's Committee on Administrative Management), p. 17.

The concession which Parliament gave, Parliament can take away. As an eminent British judge has said, if a regulation were to be framed to intern the Catholics of Ireland or the Jews of London, the result would be a speedy repeal of the Act authorizing the delegation.[30]

The first of my five conditions was that the delegation should be to a trustworthy authority commanding the national confidence. In Britain, as you may know, the most solemn form of delegated legislation is a royal proclamation or an Order in Council; our Privy Council is a very ancient rule-making authority, and several of our modern departments are offshoots of it. An Order in Council means a document in respect of which the King has formally said "approved" in the presence of three, four, or more Privy Councillors; it will usually have originated in some department other than the Privy Council. Lower in the scale are the rules, regulations, and orders made by Secretaries of State or other ministers, rules of court made by judges with the approval of the Lord Chancellor, and, near the bottom, the by-laws of municipal and other corporate bodies—which remind us that from the dawn of history the habit and practice of subordinate law-making have been indigenous in Britain. We have, of course, no such check upon the type of body to which rule-making authority is entrusted as was indicated by the Supreme Court at Washington in the Carter Coal Case in 1936.

My second condition was that the limits within which the delegated power is to be exercised ought to be defi-

[30] Lord Dunedin, in R. v. Halliday [1917] A. C. at p. 271.

nitely laid down. I meant that the control by the law-courts (by way of declaring a rule or order *ultra vires*) should be made as simple and easy as possible by inserting precise words in the enabling Act. I meant also to have suggested that the rule-making body should be obliged to state in the caption or recitals to its rules the exact statutory power which it purported to be exercising. Sometimes one sees a rule which does not give this guidance at all. Sometimes one sees such words as "The Minister of this-or-that by virtue of section so-and-so of such-and-such a statute *and all other powers him enabling* . . ." It might often be tedious and awkward to recite the pedigree of statutory powers where the rule-making authority has been transmitted through a succession of departments or is based on referential legislation. But there is a real danger that "all other powers him enabling" may baffle the seeker after knowledge and may blunt the conscious rectitude of the rule-making mind. It is the department's business to know exactly what power it is exercising. Would it be too drastic a control to enact that the rule-making authority should be estopped from relying upon any statutory power not specifically mentioned in the forefront of the rule? Perhaps so, but one cannot too strongly insist that rules and regulations should be drafted with the closest attention to the enabling power. That is a strong reason for using the services of an expert draftsman. He can see much better than a layman where the statutory tramlines are.

The challenge of rules on the ground that they are outside the powers of the enabling statutes is as valuable,

I suppose, in the United States as in Britain. The courts must go back to the statutes. In Britain they do nothing else. May I try to convey my meaning by an illustration taken rather at random from a law report of recent date?[31] The telephone service in Britain is conducted by the Post Office. A telephone subscriber disputed the number of calls for which he was charged. The Postmaster-General sued him for the few shillings in dispute and put in a certified copy of the account. The Telephone Regulations in force declare that a certified copy shall be conclusive evidence both of the amount and of the subscriber's obligation to pay it. The subscriber's counsel protested that so monstrous a regulation must be *ultra vires;* it made the Postmaster-General judge in his own cause. The English court examined the statute of 1885 under which the regulations purported to be made. The statute empowered the Postmaster-General to fix the sum to be paid and to regulate the conditions on which the telephone might be used and the general conduct of the business.[32] The regulations shrewdly began by declaring that except with the sanction of the Postmaster-General all charges should be prepaid; they went on to specify the conditions on which he would forego his insistence on prepayment; one of these conditions was the challenged provision which made the certified copy conclusive. The Court of Appeal held the disputed regulation to be *intra vires,* and the subscriber had to pay. What would not a private trader give for a privilege

[31] Wadsworth v. Postmaster-General (1939) 56 Times Law Reports, 1.

[32] See 48 & 49 Vict. c. 58, s. 2, and, for the regulations, S. R. & O. 1936, II, 3476.

making an extract from his books automatic proof of the customer's liability? I dragged in that case as one more reminder that the English courts are not concerned to see whether the enabling Act lays down standards or policy or whether it offends against the requirement of due process of law or the doctrine of the separation of powers or a constitutional rule restricting the delegation of the legislative function. Parliament being supreme in Britain, the sole question for an English court is whether the exercise of the rule-making power is within the authority prescribed in the enabling statute or not.

My third safeguard was the prior consultation of interests specially affected.[33] The duty to consult has been increasingly imposed by many British statutes in the last twenty years; there are about forty advisory councils or committees created for this purpose, some exclusively technical, like those dealing with the dyestuffs industry, or poisons, or Scottish records, others partly popular. There is no general practice of public hearings. The consultation, though genuine, is without prescribed formalities. There is, however, something like a miniature Parliament which the Minister of Transport is to consult before making regulations under the London Traffic Acts. Its forty members include representatives of government departments, the police, organized labour, London local authorities, and the councils of adjoining

[33] As regards interdepartmental consultation, it was formerly common for statutes to require one department to consult another in appropriate contexts. As constitutional theory makes the Government responsible as a whole, such directions are now often omitted. It may safely be assumed that consultations take place.

counties, and also representatives of railway and taxicab interests and the interests of persons providing or using either mechanically propelled or horse-drawn vehicles.[34] The size of this advisory body is exceptional.

Apart from these statutory requirements it is highly probable that the rule-making authority, anxious to smooth its path, will consult every available organization in advance. It is unthinkable that any important rules would be made about solicitors in England without consulting the Law Society or about doctors without consulting the British Medical Association or about local government without consulting the County Councils Association and the Association of Municipal Corporations. An official witness gave the Committee on Ministers' Powers an impressive list of the bodies consulted by the Ministry of Health before making new statutory regulations about the use of preservatives in food. Over sixty associations and individuals were notified of the draft proposals; these included various bodies representing food manufacturers, the London Chamber of Commerce, the Royal Sanitary Institute, the Society of Medical Officers of Health, and so forth. The Ministry received some thirty deputations, altered its draft in consequence at a number of points, circulated a final revised draft to three of the most important bodies, and made further amendments to meet last-minute criticisms. All this was in addition to the general duty of rule-making authorities under section 1 of the Rules Publication Act, 1893,[35] to give notice of intention to make rules and to state where copies

[34] 23 & 24 Geo. 5, c. 14, s. 58, sch. 12.

[35] 56 & 57 Vict. c. 66.

of the intended rules can be obtained. This section was passed because at that date there had been many complaints that rules (especially legal rules) were made privately with insufficient communication with interests affected and that there was no announcement about them before they actually came into force. The government draftsman became aware of pressure to insert in Bills a provision that rules should not come into force until they had lain before Parliament for a specified time. It was clear that unless something were done it might be hard to induce the House of Commons to allow departments to make rules at all or at least without some such restriction; this would often inconveniently postpone the operation of enactments. The Act therefore directed that before making certain rules at least a forty-day notice must be given of the proposal, any public body must be able to obtain copies, and the rule-making authority must take into consideration any objections before finally settling the rules. There were rather arbitrary exceptions, and special provision was necessary for speedy operation in cases of certified urgency. The Committee on Ministers' Powers recommended improvements of this Act in the light of forty-five years of experience, but nothing has yet been done.

The modern development of organized groups greatly facilitates prior consultation and prior notice. In taking advantage of it, there is the possible risk of diminishing ministerial responsibility, and the fear that the entrenched interests of big organizations will gain a disproportionate influence at the expense of ordinary inarticulate men and women. Manufacturing and selling interests exert a greater pull than the vast undrilled army of consumers.[36] The representations of employers and employees in railways or other forms of transport may drown the muttered grumbles of the unco-ordinated passengers.

My fourth safeguard was publicity. The systematic publishing of all Statutory Rules and Orders was secured in Britain by section 3 of the Rules Publication Act of 1893. The rules and orders, with some exceptions, were to be sent forthwith by the department which made them to the King's Printer (the Controller of the Stationery Office) to be by him numbered and, save as provided by regulations, printed and put on sale. The Stationery Office works in close contact with the Editor of Statutory Rules and Orders, the official already mentioned who keeps the register and supervises some of the mysteries of publication. The rules and orders are numbered in an annual series and printed in slip form with standardized subject headings such as "Customs," "Education," "Housing," "Income Tax," "Poisons," "Public Health," and so forth. Those of a general character in force at the end of a year are collected into annual volumes, the type for the slip-form prints being kept standing for this purpose. Every three years an official index to all rules and orders in force is produced; it laboriously tabulates all the statutory powers of making rules and orders and all the exercises of those powers.

[36] For the representation of consumers on the panels under the wartime Prices of Goods Act, 1939, see 2 & 3 Geo. 6, c. 118, sch. 2 par. 2.

Ever since the year of the Great Plague in the reign of Charles II, England has had the *London Gazette,* appearing twice a week, as a vehicle of official publicity. But the miscellaneous contents are so voluminous that the text of legislation is buried rather than revealed in its pages. Proclamations and Orders in Council can still be seen in the *Gazette* among the bankruptcy notices and other official advertisements; on the whole, the system of printing Statutory Rules and Orders under the 1893 Act has superseded gazetting. That system, as you know, has a parallel in the *Federal Register* of the United States. The delegated legislation of a country deserves the dignity of publication in an official series of its own, not encumbered (like the *London Gazette*) with masses of non-legislative material. In one respect the *Federal Register* has a marked advantage over the English system, because executive orders have no effect until filed for publication in the *Register.* The excellent principle "no publication, no operation" is one which Britain might adopt, as the Committee on Ministers' Powers advised.

There is a legend of Robert Browning being asked in vain in his later years to explain the meaning of one of his earlier poems. I will confess, *si parva licet componere magnis,* my doubts of what I meant in 1921 by my fifth and final safeguard, namely, that there should be machinery for amending or revoking delegated legislation as required. The outstanding characteristic and advantage of delegation is that the rules and orders can be so easily made, amended, and revoked. I must have been thinking of the checks and controls exercisable by the legislature or otherwise. As a first step the enabling Act can stipulate that the resultant rules and orders be laid before the legislature. This in itself is a feeble safeguard; [37] so many documents are laid before the House, so few are examined. Indeed it is complained that they are invisible; laying before the House means placing in the library of the House: as the custody and preservation of the document are important the document is promptly locked up and members have to ask the librarian for the key.[38] The common form of control is a provision that the delegated legislation shall take effect forthwith, but if, within a prescribed number of days [39] either House presents an adverse address, then His Majesty may by Order in Council annul the challenged document, though without prejudice to the validity of anything done under it already and without prejudice to a fresh exercise of the delegated power. This type of provision gradually established itself in place of the earlier and inconveniently dilatory requirement that a draft of the document should lie before Parliament for a prescribed number of days before taking effect. The checks and controls are of great variety; they link up with the already described arrangements for prior notice and ob-

[37] Except that it attracts section 1 (prior notice) of the Rules Publication Act, 1893, mentioned at pp. 54, 55, above. In Metcalfe v. Cox [1895] A. C. 328, the Scottish university commissioners failed to gazette and to lay before Parliament a draft ordinance. The omission was fatal.

[38] See the evidence of Sir Dennis Herbert, M. P., before the Committee on Ministers' Powers, p. 229.

[39] The number varies: it is as high as 100 days (difficult to secure in the House of Lords) in the case of certain Supreme Court Rules of Northern Ireland. See 40 & 41 Vict. c. 57, s. 69.

jection. They are not always Parliamentary. An Act of 1911 [40] allows the Minister of Transport to make an order altering the financial accounts and statistical returns which railway companies must annually submit. First the Minister must publish in the *London Gazette* a notice of his proposal, the place where copies can be obtained, and the time (one month at least) for objections to be lodged. He is to take such other steps as he thinks best adapted for informing persons affected. He must consider any objection or suggestion and must give people who make it an opportunity of communicating with him. Finally, if, before the time is up, notice is given to the Minister on behalf of companies representing at least one-third of the total aggregate capital of all the railways in the Kingdom that the companies are not satisfied with the way in which he has dealt with an objection, his order is to be "provisional" only. A "provisional order" is the technical term in Britain for one which does not take effect unless incorporated in a Bill and passed by Parliament. That seems a not inadequate check. As for the Parliamentary safeguards, we have seen some of them already. They may roughly be divided into two classes, those which operate before, and those which operate after, the document takes effect—sometimes called the pre-natal and post-natal checks. Or they may be divided according to the step which objection can take—the tolerant controls, which let the document take effect unless some prohibitory address or resolution is moved, and the more consciously applied controls, which

[40] 1 & 2 Geo. 5, c. 34, s. 3.

do not let it take effect unless some positive approval is given. Sir Dennis Herbert, in his evidence before the Committee on Ministers' Powers, thought that both the power to move an adverse address and the requirement of a confirmatory resolution were ineffective. It would seem, however, that the House of Commons could turn both these devices to good account if it cared to do so. In passing, may I add that to English eyes the comparable device in the Reorganization Act, passed by Congress last year, is extraordinarily interesting? The President makes a "plan" of reorganization and transmits it to Congress. The plan does not take effect till sixty days later, and then only if the two Houses have not passed a concurrent resolution disagreeing with it. At first sight that seems to a stranger to initiate a new phase in legislative responsibility.

The British Parliament, having delegated legislative power with increasing generosity, has its moments of misgiving when it feels it should try to exercise a sharper supervision. The horse stumbles, and the sleepy driver instinctively jerks the reins. To examine in Parliament every departmental rule, regulation, or order would defeat the very purpose of delegation; to demand, as some critics have done, that no rule, regulation, or order should take effect without an affirmative resolution would be equally impracticable. Members of Parliament, however, feel that there is a real danger that an objectionable document may escape notice. They think they should undertake some greater responsibility in scrutinizing the departmental output. The House of Lords has, under its

Standing Order 191, conscientiously remitted to a special committee all those rules, regulations, or orders which require a positive confirmatory resolution; it is determined not to pass the resolution blindly or by a mere partisan vote. This committee reports to the House whether the document raises important questions of policy, whether it is founded on precedent, and, generally, whether any further inquiry is desirable before the resolution is passed. The Committee on Ministers' Powers developed from this precedent the important recommendation that a small standing committee should be set up in each House at the beginning of each session. It would undertake a twofold scrutiny. First it would examine every Bill which proposed to delegate law-making power to a minister and would report whether the precise limits of the power were clearly defined, whether the contemplated power would involve any of those exceptional types of delegation which we discussed just now, and whether there seemed to be anything else abnormal about the proposal. This precaution would involve some delay in the legislative process: it is a just complaint by the House of Lords that Bills are in normal conditions not sent up to the Upper House in time for due consideration there before the end of the session. The scrutiny by a committee might make things worse. Moreover, the scrutiny of Bills is, after all, part of the ordinary duty of every legislator, and the number of Bills is not so huge that the task is beyond his powers; there is no reason why an objectionable clause in a Bill should slip through unnoticed. There seems much more need and justification for the second part of this scrutinizing committee's proposed functions, namely, the review of rules and regulations made under Acts. Here it was suggested that the committee should in effect report whether the delegated legislation was one of the abnormal types, whether it consisted wholly or partly of consolidation (i. e., the re-writing of existing provisions), whether it, or the circumstances in which it was made, exhibited any special feature deserving the attention of the House, and finally whether it should be starred as exceptional. If it were starred, there would be special facilities for challenging it in the House.

The general objection to this kind of scrutiny by a committee is that opponents of particular legislation would use the opportunity to renew partisan battles and to revive the opposition which had already unsuccessfully fought the policy of the statute during the Bill stage. The Committee on Ministers' Powers made it clear that the scrutinizing committee would not report upon the "merits" of rules and orders, but its proposal that the report should state "whether any matter of principle was involved" has been criticized on the ground that the distinction between "merits" and "principles" may in practice be rather fine-drawn.[41] The attitude of departmental officials towards this proposed scrutiny, so far as it can be gathered from answers in Parliament or answers before the Committee on Ministers' Powers, is respectfully sceptical. They think the plan wasteful of legislators' and

[41] See the speech of the Solicitor General, House of Commons debates, 1935, Aug. 2, col. 3088.

public servants' time in view of the mass of material to be investigated and the exclusively technical content of so much of it. The plan was based on the idea that, in putting delegated legislation through this filter, the passage of ninety-nine out of a hundred rules and orders would be unimpeded, but the hundredth instance, requiring microscopic attention, would inevitably be caught and retained. Even with expert help it is doubted whether the filter would work so automatically. It is so much easier to detect the flaw or the difficulty in rules or orders which have already been tested by actual operation than to foresee it in those which are not yet in force. In general, too, if responsibility be transferred to a committee, it must to that extent be surrendered by the Minister; the prior consultation with groups and interests might be thrown away and would be harder to conduct if the agreed results were liable to be modified by a Parliamentary committee. Either the standing committee would be tolerant and therefore otiose, or else it would be dominant and therefore constitutionally disturbing. The experiment, however, of a scrutinizing committee, or even of an independent expert official reporting to Parliament, is plainly worth trial along with any other device which might reassure the country's disquiet over alleged bureaucratic encroachments.

As things are, Parliamentary criticism and pressure provide a not inadequate safeguard. Useful understandings are reached informally in Parliamentary debates. Where an enabling Act allows rules or orders to impose a penalty for breach of their provisions, the Act now generally specifies the maximum penalty. It is becoming established that, unless the enabling Act specifically permits, the delegated legislation ought not to sub-delegate a legislative power.[42] The system of moving an adverse address against an objectionable set of regulations has proved its value. The adverse address is rarely carried, but the Minister sometimes buys off opposition by promising some modification. In 1937, for instance, the Minister of Transport made some regulations under the Road Traffic Act to ensure that automobiles did not go on the roads with inadequate brakes and tires. Some police inspection was involved; the original regulations would apparently have authorized a policeman to enter the owner's premises in his absence—an outrageous infraction of the principle that an Englishman's house is his castle. The Minister bowed gracefully to the little storm. Peace-time protests against delegated legislation admittedly proceed mainly upon party lines and are voted down out of party loyalty. The strength of war-time objections to Defence Regulations does not depend on the existence of a strong anti-war party. They have been most effectively made on the broad issue of the maintenance of personal liberty; but this and other aspects of law-making in emergency are reserved for separate consideration.

[42] See p. 88, below.

3. Crisis Legislation

I was just going to say that human beings do not ever make laws; it is the accidents and catastrophes of all kinds, happening in every conceivable way, that make the laws for us.—PLATO, LAWS, IV, 709

IF HARD cases make bad law, emergencies may make worse. Either the emergency is not allowed to disturb the permanent and immutable principles or else it smashes its way through them. On the one side are the gallant words about the Constitution of the United States used in the Milligan case:

No doctrine involving more pernicious consequences was ever invented by the wit of man than that any of its provisions can be suspended during any of the great exigencies of government. Such a doctrine leads directly to anarchy or despotism.[1]

On the other side is the maxim that public safety is the highest law of all. There is no need to repeat the fundamental difference between the American and the British conditions of law-making. In the United States the courts will tell the legislature what it cannot do; in Britain an all-powerful legislature can pass any statute without judicial challenge. And so in Britain the will of the people (if by that name one can dignify the day-to-day output of a legislature elected without any detailed or recent mandate) is the better equipped to extemporize

[1] *Ex parte* Milligan (1866) 4 Wallace, 121.

statutory measures in a crisis; but the people are left unprotected against the tyranny of the many, which can be no less repressive than the tyranny of the few.

If the British parallel be worth developing, one should perhaps add that England is a common-law country with a prerogative background. By prerogative is meant the residue of that wide executive power which the Crown, in the early days of English history, once possessed in all the departments of government, the power left with the chief magistrate "to use his discretion upon extraordinary occasions and to exercise the supreme authority in all cases where the law of the land has not directed or limited the execution." [2]

Has the President of the United States any inherent or residual powers? The executive power is expressly vested in him. He has authority as commander in chief. Professor Corwin has recently reminded us that ex-President Taft warmly protested against the notion that a President had any constitutional warrant for attempting the role of a universal Providence.[3] There are signs that the Supreme Court at Washington has glanced at the history of the British prerogative in pronouncing upon his power to pardon; but a visitor must not make the mistake of supposing that the founding fathers either said or meant that the old Adam of arbitrary monarchical absolutism should have any further survival. In Britain the official lawyers have been investigating afresh the

2 Dartmouth's note to Burnet's *History of His Own Time,* cited by Scott and Hildesley, *Case of Requisitions* (1920), p. 105. See Anson, *Law of the Constitution* (4th edition) II (Part I), 18.

3 *The President: Office and Powers* (1940), p. 132.

inherent authority to act in the face of threatened invasion. The extent is vague; but, as Maitland said, a prerogative does not cease to exist merely because it is not used. For two reasons there has been little occasion for English judges to deliver opinions upon it. First, the British Parliament usually passes an Act of Indemnity when the crisis is over. Classical writers on English constitutional law almost encourage the executive to break the law in a crisis, because the subsequent validation by statute exhibits such a triumph for the authority of the legislature. These statutory confirmations have been enacted after the conclusion of hostilities or after it has been deemed necessary to suspend the Habeas Corpus Acts in Ireland and so on.[4] Do constitutional lawyers in the United States accept as a satisfactory solution a Bill of Indemnity with its necessarily retroactive effect? Congress ratified the acts and proclamations of President Lincoln by retroactive delegation, and the Supreme Court upheld the procedure in the Prize Cases.[5]

In the second place, in Britain the legislature is constantly and cumulatively creating definite statutory powers which supersede the old indefinite prerogative. In the De Keyser's Hotel case in 1920 there was an examination of the relation of the two. A hotel in the middle of London had been requisitioned to accommodate the Royal Flying Corps headquarters. There was, within uncertain limits, an ancient right to take private

[4] See the impressive list of indemnity statutes in the judgment of Willes, J., in Phillips v. Eyre (the Jamaica case) (1870) L. R. 6 Q. B. at p. 17. See also 10 & 11 Geo. 5, c. 48.

[5] Hart, *Ordinance Making Powers of the President*, pp. 61–62, 93, etc.

property for the defence of the Realm. The Crown claimed that acting under the prerogative it paid compensation only as an act of grace; it proposed to refer the question to the Defence of the Realm Losses Commission, a tribunal set up under the prerogative. It was a perfectly fair tribunal, but the hotel owners insisted that they had a statutory right to a fair rent by way of compensation under a Defence Act of 1842. The House of Lords indorsed their contention. The Crown had been inclined to rely both on the prerogative and on any statutory rights it possessed under the Defence of the Realm Acts or otherwise; the decision established that, where a matter is dealt with both by the prerogative and by statute, and the whole of what could be done under the prerogative is covered by statutory power, it is the statute that rules.[6] The prerogative is to that extent curtailed.

Crisis legislation—to come back to it after these preliminary observations—exhibits just those faults and disadvantages which one would expect. The official draftsman would like a couple of months, if he could have them, for incubating any major legislative proposal; in time of crisis he may find himself framing some drastic change in the law with only a couple of days to do it in. Because it is hurried, it will be imperfect; because it is imperfect, it will need frequent as well as speedy amendment. Suppose that a regulation or order is to prescribe a universal black-out at night. It may direct that every lamp in a house or on a car or elsewhere must be screened

[6] *Per* Lord Dunedin [1920] A. C. 508.

or obscured so as to show the minimum of light. Will it remember to direct the painting of the bumpers of motor-vehicles with luminous paint? If this be done by order under the authority of a regulation, will the black-out regulation be wide enough to authorize the order for the white paint on vehicles? If the direction requires all vehicles to be painted, will it remember to exclude (if so intended) the vehicles which have been laid up and locked away for the duration of the war? How much light is the pedestrian to be allowed to show from a pocket torch? How will it be measured? Crisis legislation will not only be hurried, imperfect, and tentative; it will often be novel and unexpected. A Defence Regulation has suspended the Wild Birds Protection Acts in Britain so as to allow the destruction of the peregrine falcon and the taking of its eggs. What has this rare and handsome bird to do with the crisis? The answer is that it preys upon carrier pigeons. Not to wander off into a string of samples of crisis legislation, let me submit one more preliminary point of a general kind. If anyone is thinking that the extraordinarily wide powers which have been conferred on the executive in Britain in the present war show the negation and the bankruptcy of democratic liberty, there are certain considerations to the contrary. The crisis powers have been deliberately conferred by the legislature (in theory the representatives of the governed) after such normal discussion and procedure as the times permit; they are exercised with solid popular support, which is indignant at any infringement of laws necessary for the country's protection; their exercise is subject to a Parliamentary criticism and control the more constant because Parliament is almost continuously in session; their duration is temporary, and proposals for their continuance would afford a full-dress opportunity for formal objection; finally, the authority of the legislature will be invoked at the finish, as at the beginning, when the time comes to ask for the usual statutory indemnity for actions done in good faith for the reasonable purpose of defending the Realm.

Serious though they were, the technical problems of crisis government faced by President Lincoln needed less complicated legislative solution than those faced by the President in 1932. In Britain also time has not stood still. There would be something pedantic and ostrich-like in relying today, when government is founded on a popular basis, upon the old common-law dogmas so magnificently established in the age of Sir Edward Coke, when monarchical authority was the enemy. There was hot dispute in the seventeenth century over the constitutional validity of royal proclamations issued under the prerogative. Today Britain has no doubt that the prerogative is neither a valid nor a convenient instrument of large-scale lawmaking. Doubtless one could find detailed directions in proclamations issued by the Crown in former centuries. But an eminent judge declared in the De Keyser's Hotel case that there was no prerogative power to make regulations.[7] If therefore Britain wants temporary codes of law for exceptional situations, the legislature must be

[7] Lord Sumner, Att. Gen. v. De Keyser's Royal Hotel [1920] A. C. at p. 557. Cf. Lord Parker, The Zamora [1916] A. C. at p. 90.

asked to sanction them. These sanctions have followed a common pattern.

In the last thirty years there have been four major instances of Acts enabling codes of regulations to be made. The first was the Defence of the Realm Act, 1914 (afterwards extended and recast), the D. O. R. A. of the last war.[8] The second was the Restoration of Order in Ireland Act, 1920, belonging to a dismal chapter in Anglo-Irish relations and now best forgotten.[9] The third was the Emergency Powers Act, also of 1920,[10] enacted at a moment when the war-time Defence of the Realm Acts and regulations were coming to an end, and symptoms on the home front indicated that exceptional measures might still be wanted. This Act is permanent law, but it remains dormant until called into life by a proclamation of emergency. It was thus brought into operation in 1921 for the coal strike, in 1924 (for a few days only and with the minimum of publicity) for another sectional strike, and in 1926 for the general strike. A proclamation of emergency can be issued in view of an immediate threat

> . . . of such a nature and on so extensive a scale as to be calculated, by interfering with the supply and distribution of food, water, fuel or light, or with the means of locomotion, to deprive the community, or any substantial portion of the community, of the essentials of life.

---

[8] 4 & 5 Geo. 5, c. 29.

[9] 10 & 11 Geo. 5, c. 31, enabling regulations to be made for Ireland under the Defence of the Realm Consolidation Act, 1914. See Scrutton, L. J., in O'Brien's case [1923] 2 K. B. at p. 384 for vigorous comments on the method adopted. The Act is deemed abrogated as to Eire; as to Northern Ireland it is superseded by Northern Ireland statutes.

[10] 10 & 11 Geo. 5, c. 55.

The legislature inserted many powerful safeguards in this statute. The proclamation lasts only for a month at a time, but may be renewed. It must be communicated at once to Parliament. If Parliament is adjourned or prorogued, Parliament must be called together within five days. Emergency regulations may be made by Order in Council under the Act while a proclamation is in force; they do not continue in force longer than a week unless both Houses pass a resolution for their continuance. Thus, if the emergency period is a long one, the legislature has the chance to review the regulations every month. In 1921 there were three monthly continuances. In 1926, during the general strike, the state of emergency was proclaimed on April 30 and came to an end on December 19, after seven monthly continuances; the code of regulations was occasionally amended after Parliamentary debate, and as the tension lessened many regulations in the code were dropped in the final weeks. Good temper prevailed, and no lives were lost. Order being heaven's first law, this enabling Act of 1920 seems to have been accepted in Britain as a sensible weapon to keep in the cupboard. If so, a democracy is to be congratulated on having prepared itself in advance.

Lastly we come to the Emergency Powers (Defence) Act, 1939, hastily passed on the eve of the present war.[11] The use of the word "emergency" in this and other recent statutes instead of the word "war" is significant; nations cannot nowadays wait for hostilities before arming themselves with crisis powers. There have been doubts whether

[11] 2 & 3 Geo. 6, c. 62.

the legislative machine of a democracy moves fast enough in a crisis. The record of the Parliament at Westminster a year ago may be worth noting. This Act was passed in a few hours on August 24 by 457 votes to 4. Parliament met again on August 29 to hear a review of the situation. On September 1 eighteen important statutes, making emergency provision for currency, prize law, the powers of courts, new ministries, regional commissioners (who might have to take over the government of parts of the country if the centre were paralysed), military service, imports and exports, the restricted transfer of ships and aircraft, and the rights of landlords and tenants, went through. The advent of war caused six more to be passed on Sunday the 3d; by the 7th some forty statutes, mostly of a sweeping kind, had been passed, and, though the pace was too hot to last, more followed in the next few weeks. These statistics are not cited to claim merits or results for the laws enacted. Legislative speed is not to be confused with legislative efficiency, nor is it suggested that a House of Commons, containing several hundred members, can sit down and think out the necessary laws at a moment's notice. The muse of legislation does not like being called upon to strike her lyre extempore. She prefers to contemplate her themes and not to hustle her inspiration. There had been such preparation as the country's previous warnings permitted; an Air-Raid Precautions Act was passed in 1937, a Civil Defence Act (arranging for protective shelters, removal of civilians, and hospital organization) in July, 1939.[12] There were

[12] 1 & 2 Geo. 6, c. 6; 2 & 3 Geo. 6, c. 31.

the precedents of the 1914 improvisations to be improved upon. For instance, instead of leaving all questions of compensation for requisitioned property, ships, and aircraft to be raised by the cumbrous and esoteric procedure of petition of right as in the De Keyser's Hotel case, a simple statutory remedy was provided by a Defence (Compensation) Act, which set up two tribunals for assessing payments. More leisurely discussion of this proposal might have resulted in a better Act; but it has not yet been found necessary to amend it. In respect of crisis finance there was another gain from previous experience. The Government had encountered an adverse decision in 1922 in the Wilts United Dairies case,[13] in which the Food Controller was held to have acted *ultra vires* in imposing a charge of twopence per gallon as a condition of granting milk-dealers in one area a licence to buy milk imported from another area. The Emergency Powers (Defence) Act, 1939, gives the Treasury a specific power to impose and recover charges in connexion with any scheme of control authorized by Defence Regulations. These Treasury orders must be laid before the House of Commons, the legislative body concerned with taxation; they will lapse unless approved by a resolution of the House within twenty-eight days.

The 1939 Act, in authorizing the making of Defence Regulations by Order in Council, does not hamper the executive by insisting on Parliamentary approval of the codes of regulations. But it has one safeguard which was absent from the corresponding statute in 1914. It requires

[13] 38 Times Law Reports 781.

the regulations to be laid before Parliament as soon as made, and it subjects them to possible annulment if an adverse resolution is successfully moved in either House within twenty-eight days. There are teeth in this safeguard. It has led to valuable debates in which the liberty of the subject and the need of checks upon the executive have been fully asserted. There was a notable example on October 31, 1939, when there was a vigorous four-hour debate in the House of Commons on a motion for the annulment of an amending Order in Council containing many new Defence Regulations about detention, propaganda, press censorship, and curfew.[14] The Government spokesman eventually undertook that, while the new regulations must stand for the present in view of action already taken and so as not to leave a gap in the powers of the executive, the amendments should be submitted to a committee representing all parties and should be reissued in a form commanding the maximum of agreement. This was done. The curfew provisions were left untouched because it was deemed better to leave this reserve power in the hands of a Minister responsible to Parliament than to hand it over to the military authorities. The power of detention was cut down so as to apply only to persons of "hostile origin or associations" (words used in the regulations of 1914) or persons reasonably believed to have been recently concerned in prejudicial actions. Anyone so detained was to have an early chance to make representations in writing to the Home Secre-

[14] House of Commons Debates, 1939, Oct. 31, col. 1827. See also 1940, July 31, col. 1304.

tary and to be told of his right to make objections before an advisory committee; the chairman of the committee must tell him the grounds of his detention and give him such particulars as will enable him to make his defence. Moreover, the Home Secretary must make a monthly report to Parliament of the action taken under this regulation, the number of persons detained, and the number of cases in which he has not followed (for he is not obliged to follow them) the advisory committee's recommendations. The new regulation against propaganda, which spoke of any "endeavour to influence public opinion," was also cut down so as to protect honest opinion and freedom of speech. The plan for a potential press censorship was much restricted, and a power enabling a court to prohibit a convicted offender from publishing any newspaper in the United Kingdom was omitted altogether. There had been a regulation against endeavouring to "cause disaffection"; it was thought that these words might hit legitimate propaganda; the words "endeavouring to seduce from duty" were substituted. There was a regulation against sabotage, including provision against impeding the movement of any vessel or vehicle; words were introduced to make it clear that nobody would be guilty of this offence by reason only of his peacefully taking part in a strike. That rather tedious recital of verbal changes may persuade you that even in war-time the House of Commons was at that date still well able to insist on the mitigation of drastic powers capable of arbitrary exercise and to intervene to protect the expression of extreme and unpopular opinions. The extent of that protection is one of the criteria of freedom. "It is indeed one test of belief in principles," said an eminent British judge, "if you apply them to cases with which you have no sympathy at all; you really believe in freedom of speech if you are willing to allow it to men whose opinions seem to you wrong and even dangerous." [15]

As emergencies are seen to be intensified, there is naturally a greater need and readiness to tighten up the law. The original Defence of the Realm Act in 1914 had a modest beginning. It was recommended to Parliament as necessary because special courts might be wanted for cases of tapping wires or attempts to blow up bridges.[16] Few then foresaw the forest of regulations and orders which were to spring up in the following years. The 1939 Act similarly began quietly. It refrained from modernizing the archaic law of treason, with its complicated procedure and its hazards of interpretation, which caused so much trouble at the trial of Roger Casement in 1916. This omission has been made good by the passing of a Treachery Act last May, creating a new offence punishable with death on conviction obtained under the normal procedure prescribed for trials for felony.[17] The original Emergency Powers (Defence) Act of 1939 made three reservations. No Defence Regulation was to authorize (i) any form of compulsory naval, military, or air-force service; (ii) any form of industrial conscription; or (iii) the

[15] Lord Justice Scrutton, in O'Brien's case [1923] 2 K. B. at p. 382.

[16] House of Commons Debates, Aug. 7, 1914, col. 2192.

[17] 3 & 4 Geo. 6, c. 21. A Defence Regulation has temporarily superseded the right of peremptory challenge of jurors in treason and felony trials.

trial by court martial of any person other than those subject to the special statutes which govern the navy, army, and air force.

These three reservations have been gradually whittled down. Compulsory military service was dealt with by an *ad hoc* statute ten days later.[18] Industrial conscription was brought nearer by a Control of Employment Act,[19] which in turn was superseded by an amending Emergency Powers (Defence) Act, already mentioned,[20] which, in the widest possible terms, authorized the making of Defence Regulations whereby everyone in Britain could be required to place himself, his services, and his property at the disposal of His Majesty. The restriction on trying civilians by court martial was relaxed by the Treachery Act in the case of enemy aliens.[21]

Enemy action may require departure from the slow and stately processes of peace-time criminal justice. If invasion or destruction relax law and order and release the normal restraints upon violence and theft, the leisurely committal of the accused to the next assizes and binding over witnesses to appear there will be impracticable. An Emergency Powers (Defence) Act (No. 2), passed last August,[22] authorizes the creation by Defence Regulations of special "war-zone" courts "where, by reason of recent or immediately apprehended enemy action, the military situation is such as to require that criminal justice should

18 2 & 3 Geo. 6, c. 81. 19 2 & 3 Geo. 6, c. 104.

20 3 & 4 Geo. 6, c. 20. See pp. 19, 20, above.

21 A provision for an alternative method of carrying out the death penalty seems to be due to memories of the fate of Major André in 1780.

22 3 & 4 Geo. 6, c. 45.

be administered more speedily than would be practicable by the ordinary courts."

As I have been suggesting that the British legislature has not lost control of the executive in a time of crisis, let me add that it would have been legally permissible to create these special tribunals by a Defence Regulation. The Government preferred to ask Parliament to do it by statute. Examination of the Parliamentary time-table suggested that the Government expected to get its Bill through both Houses in two days. Actually it took a fortnight. One amendment, proposed in the House of Lords, sought to insist that the regulations for these special courts should not take effect unless approved by a resolution of both Houses, instead of taking effect forthwith subject to annulment on an adverse address. This was rightly rejected; it would have been too slow a process to let ingenious critics range over several pages of draft regulations line by line, with the possibility of different amendments in the two Houses and the consequent risk of having to start with a new Order in Council all over again. Parliament debated the Bill thoroughly and inserted several safeguards, including a stipulation that death sentences should be reviewed by high judicial authorities.

May I here return to what has already been said about the inherent common-law powers which exist in Britain *in furore belli,* when war is raging? The loose phrase "martial law" is, of course, to be distinguished from "military law," which is the statutory code governing the army. "Martial law" means that the ordinary government of the country is suspended and exceptional powers are in consequence assumed. The exceptional powers do not depend on any preliminary proclamation of "martial law" but on the circumstances of the case; the proclamation is just a useful warning that things have gone too far for anything else. Military courts are then set up which upon examination turn out not to be courts at all; prohibition will not issue to control their proceedings; [23] the ordinary law courts refuse to interfere; the actions of the military authorities *in furore belli* are not "justiciable." It is illusory to find in these tribunals, administering justice under the supervision of a military commander, any analogy to the regular proceedings of ordinary courts of justice.[24] Stephen, the historian of English criminal law, described these tribunals as merely "committees" formed for the purpose of carrying into execution the discretionary powers assumed by the Government.[25] In the corresponding circumstances of the Milligan case it was insisted that the invasion must be real; the courts must be closed and the civil administration deposed. Congress could not invest military commissioners with jurisdiction to try citizens for offences in a state not invaded and not in rebellion—a state in which the federal courts were open. In the South African war the Privy Council in England held that the sitting of some civil courts for some purpose did not show that war was not raging.[26] Be that

[23] *In re* Clifford and O'Sullivan [1921] 2 A. C. 570.

[24] Tilonko v. Att. Gen. of Natal [1907] A. C. 95.

[25] *History of Criminal Law,* I, 216, approved in R. v. Allen [1921] 2 Irish Reports, 241.

[26] *Ex parte* Marais [1902] A. C. 109. Sir Frederick Pollock's note on Lord Halsbury's statement, at pp. 115–16, is interesting.

as it may, the broad result is that if the sentence of the military tribunal is one of death and it is carried out, there is an end of it. But if it is a ten-year imprisonment and conditions become normal and no Act of Indemnity is passed, the military action can be challenged before a jury when peace arrives. The creation of the new special "war-zone courts" by the recent statute in Britain may be a further cramping of the free hand of the military or the executive in crisis, a further curtailment of prerogative power by Parliamentary intervention.

Apart from these developments in the criminal law there has been a general authority under an Administration of Justice (Emergency Provisions) Act [27] to make elastic arrangements for the sittings and jurisdiction of courts and for the exercise of the powers to make rules or orders, so that the Lord Chancellor (or, if necessary, some other judge nominated for the purpose) can adapt the whole forensic system to the requirements of unforeseen crises. Civil litigation in England has been taken care of by a Courts (Emergency Powers) Act [28] similar to a statute passed in the previous war. It gives a sort of moratorium. Remedies cannot be enforced without leave of the court. The judge has to decide whether inability to pay a debt is due to circumstances caused by the war or to some other human disinclination. There was doubt whether this statute applied to the Crown—for instance, whether its protection could be invoked against an income-tax de-

[27] 2 & 3 Geo. 6, c. 78.

[28] 2 & 3 Geo. 6, c. 67; for a typical case under it see Brandon v. Reidy (1940) 56 T. L. R. 467; see also *ibid.*, p. 837.

mand. It has been held that it does not bind the Crown.[29]

If there be any question whether to use the method of a statute or the method of a Defence Regulation, it has to be remembered that Defence Regulations are not capable of everything. They cannot, for instance, have retrospective effect. And, though I have hitherto been speaking of the control of them by the legislature, we must certainly not forget the control by the judicature. There was a reminder of this last August when Mr. Justice Bennett held part of Defence Regulation 55 to be *ultra vires*.[30] This is the regulation which authorizes the general control of industry. The orders of the Ministry of Supply for controlling all sorts of things (aluminium, petroleum, iron and steel, paper, wool, and so forth), the orders of the Ministry of Food for rationing food, controlling prices, and obtaining returns about stocks, and the orders of the Board of Trade rationing motor fuel, were among those made under the early part of Regulation 55. These were unaffected by the decision which related only to the power under paragraph 4 for a competent authority to carry on (or to authorize somebody to carry on) an existing undertaking, trade, or business. Anybody thus put in to carry on a business was to be deemed the agent of the owners. The manager of a tool-making company complained that on July 17 he received from the Ministry of Supply a document telling him that, as the competent authority, the Minister had authorized two men named in the document to carry on his business: he said that soon

[29] Att. Gen. v. Hancock [1940] 1 K. B. 427.

[30] E. H. Jones (Machine Tools) Ltd. v. Farrell and Muirsmith, *The Times*, Aug. 3, 9, 14, 1940.

afterwards his bank informed him that it had received instructions to "freeze" all the company's accounts. An answer in Parliament showed that persons had thus been appointed to take charge of private business in eleven cases. The judge's decision was that the challenged paragraph exceeded the powers conferred by the enabling Act on the rule-making authority. If the regulation were valid, there seemed no limit to the extent to which the two new men could pledge the undertaking's credit or disregard the statutory limits on a company's activity. He held the paragraph *ultra vires.* This paragraph was at once withdrawn and replaced by another which made the appointees the agents of the Crown, not the agents of the persons to whom the business belonged; it also cut down the powers of the appointees. Mr. Jones said he was quite satisfied with the new paragraph and could not challenge its validity.

On the other hand, in September the court rejected an attack on a Defence Regulation under which an Englishman had been detained on account of his association with a suspected organization. This had been a difficult regulation to draft. Under it the Home Secretary could detain persons if he had reasonable cause to believe them to be members of, or to be or to have been active in furthering the objects of, an organization in respect of which the Home Secretary was satisfied that (*a*) the organization was subject to foreign interest or control or (*b*) the persons in control were in sympathy with the system of government of a power with which His Majesty was at war. As already mentioned, there was to be an advisory committee.[31] Mr. Lees was given the prescribed statement, containing reasons for his detention, by the advisory committee; it included an allegation that he had expressed pro-Fascist views. He applied for *habeas corpus;* he said he was not a Fascist—he had been for twenty-three years a Crown servant and, when arrested, was waiting to embark to take up a public post overseas. The Home Secretary made an affidavit that he had carefully studied the reports and had come to the conclusion that there were clear grounds for believing him to be a member of an organization and to have been active in furthering its objects within the terms of the regulation. The judges said in effect, "We have power to inquire into the validity of the detention order and for that purpose to ascertain if the Home Secretary had reasonable ground for the belief expressed in the order." Having considered the Home Secretary's affidavit, the court accepted his statements and was satisfied that he had reasonable cause: he was bound to act on information supplied to him; the information was necessarily confidential; to disclose it to Mr. Lees and to the public and to name the persons who supplied it might well be prejudicial to the State. The *habeas corpus* application was dismissed.[32] Mr. Lees had been released before his appeal came on. The Crown denied that this was an admission that the detention was improper; the Home Secretary had suspended the detention order—he had not cancelled it. It was contended for Mr. Lees that such affidavits of reasonable belief by the Home Secretary would make *habeas corpus* useless.

[31] See pp. 75–76, above.

[32] *The Times,* Sept. 10, 1940.

A perfectly innocent and patriotic person, however wrongly detained, would have no remedy. One Lord Justice said he thought the detention order might be held bad if the Home Secretary made an obvious blunder; but if the Home Secretary swore that he had materials before him which he had considered, it would take very strong evidence to establish that he had no reasonable cause. Counsel for Mr. Lees rejoined that even then it would be easy for the authorities to make a fresh regulation giving the Home Secretary an absolute discretion. That may be true; but that is where the legislature would have to interfere. The Court of Appeal held the existing regulation valid; the Home Secretary honestly believed with reasonable cause that the applicant was of the character described in the regulation; the detention order was good, and *habeas corpus* would not apply.[33]

The issue is not always as high as personal liberty. Short of that, there are many questions which do not reach the courts when war is raging. "Experience must have taught us all," said Lord Sumner in the De Keyser's Hotel case,[34] "that many things are done in the name of the executive in such times, purporting to be for the common good, which Englishmen have been too patriotic to contest." Another common-law judge, never a fulsome admirer of government departments, made the classic remark that war cannot be carried on according to the principles of Magna Carta; there must be some modification of the liberty of the subject in the interests of the State.[35] Natu-

[33] *The Times*, Oct. 3, 1940.

[34] [1920] A. C. at p. 557.

[35] Lord Justice Scrutton in Ronnfeldt v. Phillips (1918) 35 T. L. R. at p. 47.

rally the judges will not tell the executive how to conduct a war. "Those who are responsible for the national security must be the sole judges of what the national security requires. It would be obviously undesirable that such matters should be made the subject of evidence in a court of law or otherwise discussed in public." [36] When the issue is the validity of an order for the internment of a person "of hostile origin or associations" the English judges have said that "no tribunal for investigating the question whether circumstances of suspicion exist warranting some restraint can be imagined less appropriate than a court of law." [37]

In most of the cases where Defence Regulations and orders were challenged during the last war and the years that followed, the attack failed; but three cases indicated certain limits to the scope within which the delegated power could be exercised. In 1920 the Shipping Controller's power to requisition shipping was held not to justify requisitioning the service of owners and their staffs.[38] In *Chester v. Bateson* a regulation designed to make sure that there was accommodation for munition workers forbade landlords to take action without consent of the Minister of Munitions for recovering possession of dwellings so occupied.[39] The judges said that the enabling statute could not have gone so far as to forbid access to the courts in such a case; so grave an invasion of the rights of all subjects was not intended by the legisla-

[36] Lord Parker in the Zamora case [1916] 2 A. C. at p. 107.
[37] Lord Finlay, L. C., in R. v. Halliday [1917] A. C. at p. 269.
[38] China Mutual Steam Navigation Co. v. Maclay [1918] 1 K. B. 33.
[39] [1920] 1 K. B. 829.

ture to be accomplished by a departmental order of the Minister of Munitions; it could be done, of course, by Act of Parliament. We seem here to be on the edge of a judicial pronouncement that there are certain fundamental rights which legislation cannot diminish—the American rather than the British doctrine. The decision has been criticized by those who think that a regulation for housing munition workers was sufficiently connected with the national defence to be within the powers of the enabling statute; if so, it did not matter whether the provision was in a statute or a regulation; the regulation, if *intra vires,* would have the same strength as the statute, and the order, if properly made under the regulation, would be valid. We may note that in the present war a Defence Regulation provides for carrying on a business in the public interest even though the business constitutes a statutory nuisance; [40] if the competent authority makes an order authorizing particular work to go on in a particular place, the regulation prevents anyone from taking legal proceedings; a court therefore cannot be asked to grant an injunction. The third defeat for a government department was the Newcastle Breweries case in 1920, where rum had been requisitioned. It was held that the legislature did not contemplate regulations which withheld fair compensation for goods taken.

It is an established rule that a statute will not be read as authorising the taking of a subject's goods without payment unless the intention to do so is clearly expressed; this rule must apply no less to partial than to total confiscation,

[40] Defence (General) Regulations 54A (S. R. & O. 1940 No. 697).

and it must apply *a fortiori* to the construction of a statute delegating legislative powers.[41]

You will have noticed that the four big enabling statutes to which I have referred have the common feature that the resultant codes of regulations do not tell the whole story. There is not only delegation of the legislative power, but also sub-delegation. If so, what about the maxim *delegata potestas delegari non potest?* Legal scholarship has suggested that the maxim originated in a historic misunderstanding; [42] none the less the English courts respect its principle, and the modern draftsman bears it in mind. For one thing, if a statute delegates power to a minister to make a regulation with prescribed formalities of prior notice or consultation, it would be unsatisfactory if the minister could redelegate to himself a power to legislate without such formalities. Examination of the enabling Defence of the Realm Acts of the last war does not reveal any express authority for His Majesty in Council, when making Defence of the Realm Regulations, to redelegate his legislative power to a government department or other body. Yet this sub-delegation or redelegation was common and resulted in copious orders, the grandchildren of the Act, which were sometimes more important to the obedient citizen than the regulations which were themselves the children of the Act. Nobody seems to have challenged this sub-delegation in the last war as being *ultra vires.* When we come to the enabling Act of the present war, we find that the draftsman has

41 [1920] 1 K. B. 866.
42 Duff and Whiteside, 14 *Cornell Law Quarterly* (1929), p. 168.

inserted a specific and comprehensive sanction for Defence Regulations to empower any specified authorities or persons to make orders, rules, and by-laws for any of the purposes for which the regulations themselves might have been made.[43] He has not left any doubt about it, and, although draftsmen often insert words *ex abundanti cautela,* his express provision here indicates that he thought the grandchildren might otherwise be illegal. He also provides that both the children and the grandchildren shall take effect notwithstanding anything inconsistent therewith contained in any enactment other than the enabling Act itself. The Defence Regulations, by the way, have played havoc with the statute-book, suspending, amending, and restricting Acts of Parliament right and left; but in practice the grandchildren have not been allowed to do this. I would add that it is understood to be the custom for all the Defence Regulations, the direct children of the Act, to be drafted by, or at any rate approved and passed on to the Privy Council by, the official Parliamentary Counsel who are in a sense independent of any government department. And it is understood that, except in trivial or specially urgent cases, all Defence Regulations go before the Home Policy Committee of the Cabinet. These steps and stages give no small opportunity for criticism and control.

[43] See 2 & 3 Geo. 6, c. 62, s. 1(3). Compare s. 2(1) of the Emergency Powers Act, 1920 (10 & 11 Geo. 5, c. 55), s. 1(2) of the National Economy Act, 1931 (21 & 22 Geo. 5, c. 48), and s. 2 of the Air Navigation Act, 1936 (26 Geo. 5 & 1 Edw. 8, c. 44). There was complaint of the sub-delegation in the Air Navigation Order: see Sir W. Graham Harrison's evidence before the Committee on Ministers' Powers, p. 50 (question 700).

Some of the Defence Regulations of the present war, the children of the 1939 Act, are self-contained. They definitely create criminal offences—looting, for instance (punishable with death), sabotage (punishable with fourteen years penal servitude), action to assist the enemy, communication with enemy agents, signalling, and so forth. But other regulations give blank powers which are to be filled in by ministerial orders, the grandchildren of the Act. What is your duty in England to black out the lights in your house? Defence Regulation 24 merely says that the Secretary of State may by order provide for prohibiting or regulating the display of lights. You must look at the Lighting (Restriction) Order, made under Regulation 24. Have you a motor-car? Listen to Regulation 19A:

> A Secretary of State or the Minister of Home Security may by order provide for requiring mechanically propelled road vehicles . . . to be rendered, when not being driven, incapable of use by unauthorised persons during such hours as may be so specified . . .

Again you must make the acquaintance of the grandchild. Are you in what is called an evacuation area? Your movements will be governed by orders under Regulation 21. Have you land? Its use will be subject to directions of the Minister of Agriculture and Fisheries issued under Regulation 62, which authorizes the control of cultivation. Control of navigation, motor-fuel rationing, food control, and all sorts of other activities are governed by orders made under blank powers in regulations. During the last war, by the way, these grandchildren were not registered, numbered, and printed in the official series of what we call Statutory Rules and Orders in the general scheme of official publishing under the Rules Publication Act, 1893,[44] which is roughly parallel to your Federal Register Act. The view was held that the words prescribing official publication in the 1893 Act, when they mention "rules, regulations or by-laws made under any Act of Parliament," must mean those made directly under an Act, not those made at one remove—the children, not the grandchildren. In the present war the grandchildren have been included in the same system as their immediate parents, that is to say, they are published separately in the official slip-form system and issued as S. R. & O. 1939 No. so-and-so or S. R. & O. 1940 No. so-and-so, and published also collectively in the annual volumes at the end of the year. One result of including these grandchildren is to send up the annual total of Statutory Rules and Orders, but the increase is partly offset by a drop in the normal output of departments whose public services have been damped down by war-time preoccupations. The Defence Regulations and orders come out in a great hurry; with the best will in the world it is not easy to issue them to the public as promptly as one would desire. The need of preliminary secrecy is a minor cause of delay. Some of them are kept secret under special direction. Orders relating to "protected places" which the public must not enter are in this class.[45] To publish a list of the areas would give useful information to the enemy.

[44] 56 & 57 Vict. c. 66.

[45] See Defence (General) Regulations 12(5), 14(2), 54C(6), 84A(5), and the Defence (Evacuation Areas) Regulations 3(2).

In the eternal dispute between government and liberty, crisis means more government and less liberty. I end as I began by saying that, while the Anglo-Saxon tradition keeps alive historic suspicions of legislation by an encroaching executive, there is also the possibility of tyranny by the legislature itself. Democracy, as we have seen, needs and improvises exceptional weapons against exceptional attacks. Free peoples, when they temporarily surrender freedom, will expect to see their inheritance restored to them when the storm is over. There will be two anxious questions—how large must that surrender be, and how soon will the restoration come? Intensive regimentation and restrictions, impatient suppression of heterodox views, internment of dissentients, and other phenomena likely to be visible in times of grave stress are steps towards dictatorship, even when taken along a lawful and constitutional road. The most successful dictator is he who gains his power without forsaking that road. Hence the anxiety. Yet laws and constitutions are but the paper safeguards of liberty. A people must have the will to be free.

4. Administrative Tribunals

A host of controversies as to private rights are no longer decided in courts.—CHIEF JUSTICE HUGHES

ADMINISTRATIVE adjudication has been receiving the attention it deserves. The Lord Chancellor of England made it one of the subjects of inquiry entrusted to the Committee on Ministers' Powers in 1929. To that committee it seemed the major threat against the Rule of Law because in England, as Dicey had explained,

> any encroachment on the jurisdiction of the courts and any restriction on the subject's unimpeded access to them are bound to jeopardise his rights to a much greater degree than would be the case in a country like the United States where they are protected by the express terms of a written constitution.

In the United States there have been several investigations. The American Bar Association has shown a far more active interest than the General Council of the Bar would show in England. The legal practitioner is naturally perturbed by procedural diversities and anomalies which he has not always the means or the enthusiasm to master; he hopes for standardization based on the forensic routine with which he is familiar. The President's Committee on Administrative Management has studied the "independent regulatory commissions" in the hope of finding some means of making them both politically responsible and judicially independent. It seeks to "break down" the functions of a commission so as to divide the administrative and policy-forming from the judicial or quasi-judicial. It sees the danger of bodies acting both as prosecutor and as judge. The examination on behalf of the Attorney-General's committee (with which Professor Gellhorn is identified) and the somewhat similar inquiry by Mr. Benjamin as Moreland commissioner at the instance of the Governor of New York State are at the moment *sub judice*. Any coincident recommendations resulting from these two explorations will carry the weight due to the care and thought devoted to them. Serious study will avoid the mistake of supposing that a single universal formula for all kinds of tribunals offers an easy solution. In England, as perhaps in the United States, few champions are nowadays found to maintain that the only remedy is the abolition of all administrative adjudication and the assignment of all the obnoxious jurisdictions to the ordinary courts.

The history of Anglo-American jurisprudence has established the significance of "unimpeded access" to the law-courts; but, as we take a random glance at the earlier pages, we see the courts enjoying no monopoly. In medieval times the men who were united in gilds and fraternities bound themselves by the principle that they should not take domestic quarrels into court without first trying, like good brothers, to have them settled within the brotherhood.[1] This habit had to be checked by statute in 1503,[2] when gilds, fraternities, and companies corporate were forbidden to make any ordinances restrain-

[1] Gross, *Gild Merchant*, I, 65.

[2] 19 Hen. 7, c. 7, s. 2.

ing persons from suing to the King's courts for due remedy. The habit was hard to break. An Elizabethan chartered company, the Mineral and Battery Works, in effect a munition-producing undertaking of the Armada period, had a rule that no member was to sue a fellow-member in debt or trespass, but that all such disputes were to be submitted to the judgment of the society.[3] Besides corporate privileges of self-government there was another influence, the familiar desire of the merchants to decide their disputes in their own way. The ordinance of the Staple had warned off the King's justices.[4] To the commercial community arbitration has long been a welcome alternative to the procedure of the regular courts. An Act of Elizabeth set up a special tribunal for marine insurance.[5] It recites the custom of the merchants to have their insurance disputes settled by certain grave and discreet merchants appointed by the Lord Mayor of London; lately, however, divers persons have "withdrawn themselves from that arbitrary course" (which means that course of arbitration) "and have sought to draw the parties assured to seek their moneys of every several assurer by suits commenced in Her Majesty's courts, to their great charges and delays." The Act authorizes the Lord Chancellor to set up a standing commission to determine these disputes "in a brief and summary course . . . without formalities of pleadings or proceedings." The Admiralty judge was to be a member; so was the recorder of London. There were also to be two doctors of the civil

[3] *Select Charters of Trading Companies,* Selden Society, XXVIII, xcviii.
[4] 27 Edw. 3, stat. 2, c. 1, ss. 5, 8.
[5] 43 Eliz. c. 12: see also 14 Car. 2, c. 23.

law, two common lawyers, and eight grave and discreet merchants. The quorum would be five. In spite of the judicial element in its constitution, the common-law courts managed to stifle this intruder in the end.[6]

That strong spirit of corporate self-discipline among the fraternities survives in various professional organizations in England today. Statute has largely replaced charter in recognizing and confirming it. There are domestic tribunals for doctors and dentists and lawyers and architects, as also for midwives and nurses. There is no uniformity. The jurisdiction of the English Inns of Court over a barrister, empowering them to "disbar" a member and thus deprive him of his livelihood, is subject to appeal to the judges as "visitors" of the Inns, but has no statutory foundation. The right of the General Medical Council to strike a practitioner's name off the medical register either for a criminal conviction (which is definite enough) or for "infamous conduct in any professional respect" (which is much more vague and controversial) is a statutory right, but is not subject to appeal unless the members of the tribunal had no evidence on which to found their decision or have fallen short in "natural justice"—whereof more anon. All the more recent statutes, when they create a professional tribunal, give a right of appeal therefrom to the courts.

These domestic and other jurisdictions were not developed upon any logical plan. It is doubtful whether the inherent advantages of an extra-judicial tribunal—speed and cheapness, for instance, and procedural sim-

[6] See Holdsworth, *History of English Law*, VIII, 290.

plicity and the availability of specialized knowledge —were consciously studied. Bentham in his *Constitutional Code* early placed on record the advantages which the presence of judges can confer. He proposed that in disputes between citizens and ministers a judge might be called in to improve the eliciting of evidence and to avoid the appearance or suspicion of favour or disfavour and for publicity. In the common-law countries, with their immemorial tradition of corporate life, authority and responsibility have been committed to laymen whom the old charters describe as "grave and discreet," "merchants of good credit and reputation," and so on. Such men, acting in full view of their fellows and fortified perhaps by some oath or declaration of fidelity to the common cause, seldom disappointed the confidence reposed in them. There would be as little expectation of bias as there is when the annual University Boat Race on the Thames is umpired by either an Oxford or a Cambridge man. Belief that the judges are the sole repositories of incorruptibility must be a modern growth. Which tribunal would an Elizabethan citizen have preferred, if invited to choose between Francis Bacon and the Lord Mayor of London? Today there is perhaps a fuller consciousness of the value of the maxim that justice not only must be done but must also manifestly be seen to be done. That refinement of the common notions of fair play we owe to the judges.

I must not try your patience with accounts of our quasi-judicial bodies in Britain. In railway affairs we have seen jurisdiction offered to the law-courts (amid the protests of judges that they were being turned into railway directors) and afterwards transferred elsewhere. Workmen's compensation has been retained in the ordinary courts in Britain, but other jurisdictions involving the discretionary application of policy have found tribunals of their own. The material for any investigation into quasi-judicial activities is bound to be more copious in the United States. If it be there found possible to disentangle the judicial from the administrative element in governmental agencies and to keep law and policy apart, we shall be watching with interest from Britain. As in the delegation of legislative power, it is a question of convenience and confidence; and confidence is a question of human competence.

Besides the issues of law and policy there are also issues of fact. It will narrow the scope of our discussion (will it not?) if we can agree that simple questions of fact can be determined cheaply, swiftly and acceptably outside the law-courts—questions, for instance, of the assessment of compensation when some Naboth's vineyard is wanted for public purposes. Naboth, of course, may be more deeply interested to retain his vineyard than to contest the figure of compensation. We are taking it for granted that the country, through the legislature, has decided that private vineyards are less important than some supposed public need, but that expropriated vineyard-owners shall be compensated. The Naboths must accept that decision. If the basis of compensation is settled, is not the price-fixing mere fact-finding? Two statutes were passed in the same session of Elizabeth, one for improving Plymouth harbour, the other for making a channel to connect Chichester with the sea. Each contemplates a trench being dug and compensation being paid to the landowner. In the Plymouth case the figure is to be assessed by the two judges of the Devon assizes, in the Chichester case by a commission of twelve, four to be aldermen or discreet citizens of Chichester and the other eight to be noblemen or gentlemen in the commission of the peace of the county of Sussex.[7] Is the judicial tribunal in the Plymouth case right and is the lay tribunal in the Chichester case wrong? As further social or other needs have arisen for expropriating private vineyards, whether for water supply or in the course of either the canal mania of the seventeen-nineties or the railway mania of the eighteen-forties, Naboth has found himself with varying tribunals to which to apply for compensation. There was a sensible standardization in England in 1848; each side could appoint an arbitrator, and the arbitrators could appoint an umpire. In 1919 a statute created a panel of official arbitrators with special knowledge of land valuation. A Reference Committee, consisting of the Lord Chief Justice, the Master of the Rolls, and the President of the Surveyors' Institution, could select a man from the panel to decide any dispute about compensation where land is acquired compulsorily for public purposes. These cases need no longer stir up controversy over the right of access to the courts. The chief occasion for bitterness arises over land taken in the course of

[7] 27 Eliz. cc. 20 and 22. For earlier precedents on each side see 31 Hen. 8, c. 4 (Exeter navigation) and 13 Eliz. c. 18 (River Lea).

housing improvement, where Naboth's compensation award may be reduced in value because the existing premises are insanitary and unfit for human habitation. Nobody likes to be branded as a slum-owner as well as losing compensation on that account. The fairness of the treatment and the requirements of public health are alike in dispute on such occasions. Lord Sumner characteristically illustrated this quarrel in *Hall v. Manchester Corporation.*[8] The appellant's case, he said, was that he and his houses had been condemned unheard, that he had been manœuvred out of his right of appeal, that he was mulcted for a sanitarian's counsel of perfection, and that what was good enough for our fathers should be good enough for us. We may add that, in so far as these sentiments represent the rearguard fight of *laissez-faire,* it is the legislature, quite as much as the executive, which is the enemy.

Though the preference for the law-courts may be due to the fear that any other tribunal will not be fair, the Committee on Ministers' Powers received plenty of independent testimony in favour of the fairness of departmental tribunals, or at any rate of the government officials who hold local inquiries. It is not at all certain that administrative tribunals are unpopular in England. Men concerned with railway matters would as soon go before the Minister of Transport as before a judge. To the administrator the disadvantage of the law-courts is that judicial decisions are not uniform. To save the time of the High Court in England, statutes confer as much juris-

[8] (1915) 84 L. J., N. S. (Ch.), at p. 744.

diction as possible upon the judges of the county courts. There are some sixty of these judges, men appointed for their high standing at the bar. They have independent minds and cannot produce unified decisions. Variety of judicial determination was understood to be the reason why jurisdiction in national health insurance, originally entrusted to the county court judges, was afterwards transferred to a department. Legal chairmen of this type were employed in the classification of aliens in Britain at the beginning of the present war. Some of these aliens tribunals, it is said, awarded mostly "Class B" certificates, others mostly "Class C." They were impartial; they were not uniform. This human diversity must be reckoned with where classification is separately undertaken in a new field.

Often a non-judicial tribunal commends itself to public opinion in Britain because a judge is appointed to preside. It is unsatisfactory to grade the tribunal according to the profession of the persons constituting it. In considering what sort of tribunal is required, one must have regard to the subject awaiting decision. Will there be some core of law on which judicial teeth could bite, some body of general principles which judicial minds could apply? Or will considerations of policy predominate? If there is a question under the housing statutes whether a dwelling is or is not reasonably fit for human habitation, who ought to decide it? No issue is too technical for a court. "Reasonably fit" suggests a jury because it involves the standard of ordinary reasonable men.[9]

[9] Reasonable fitness was said to be a judicial question (the housing

Judges and juries, or judges sitting alone, manage to cope with all sorts of conundrums, aided either by assessors or by expert witnesses. It does not follow that it is worth while to occupy the courts with every question under the sun—whether, for instance, a tomato is a fruit or a vegetable for tariff purposes, or whether linoleum is furniture for the purpose of a landlord's charge to a tenant, or whether the Municipal Civil Service Commissioners of New York wrongly deprived candidates of qualifying marks for an answer about punctuation in an examination paper.[10] The judges themselves are not always anxious to assert their jurisdiction. There are many matters, said Lord Sumner in *Roberts v. Hopwood*,[11] which the courts are indisposed to question; though they are the ultimate judges of what is lawful and what is unlawful to borough councils, they often accept the decision of the local authority "because they themselves are ill equipped to urge the merits of one solution of a practical question against another."

It hardly seems right to assign to the courts an issue involving the promotion of housing or public health without taking account of statutory developments which impose on departments the duty to promote a better stand-

---

order carried a penalty if disregarded) in Hall v. Manchester Corporation, *ibid.*, pp. 742–43.

[10] The question was whether a note of interrogation (instead of a full stop) should come at the end of the test words, "May I help you with your problem of reorganisation of the personnel." See Bruno v. Kern, *New York Law Journal*, Sept. 13, 1940, p. 612. The court said "Yes."

[11] [1925] A. C. 606.

ard. Somehow the level of reasonable fitness in housing has been raised perceptibly in England in the last thirty years. This is not due to action by the courts. There are local variations; what is good enough for one place is not good enough for another. As in Chadwick's day, some central authority must work to lift the low local standard to the reasonably high uniform level. The legislature puts this duty on the administrators, not on the judges. If the legislature allows the administrators a discretion, it gives them a power to be arbitrary. Will it try to stipulate that the decision is not to be arbitrary? Will it say, for instance, that the decision shall be final if supported by evidence, or if supported by "substantial evidence"? And, if no such words are used, will the courts still find themselves able to intervene because there has not been due process of law? Or will there be no control of arbitrariness except by control of appointment and of promotion? The courts seem disinclined to review the correctness of an administrative determination where the power to determine is lawfully present. The element of adjudication, of course, may be very slight. In Britain in the last war the Home Secretary had power to make orders deporting aliens. Was it enough that he thought they were aliens, or had he to address his mind to the matter judicially? He was held not to be a judicial officer for the purpose, but an executive officer; he was not bound to hold an inquiry or to hear the persons affected. The position in the United States is different. To deport as an alien a man who claims to be a citizen will be an obvious occasion for invoking the protection of the Fifth Amendment in its guarantee of due process of law.[12]

The finality of a simple administrative decision is shown in a recent English case. The corporation of Newcastle-upon-Tyne had statutory power to erect railings on the edge of pavements to protect pedestrians from traffic dangers. Its decision where to put the railings was essentially administrative. Shopkeepers whose frontage was affected protested in the courts in vain. If the corporation did anything so ridiculous as to put up a close-boarded fence ten feet high along the pavement, said Lord Justice Goddard, the frontagers might well ask the court to say that the power exercised was not the power granted..

> But I do not think that this court or any other court has any right to canvass the decision of a local authority on a matter which Parliament has placed in their hands to decide. It is not a question whether the Ministry of Transport or the police or the watch committee took this view or that view. It is a question entirely for the corporation as a corporation to decide, and, they having come to a decision with regard to this matter, it is not open that the length or extension of this fence should be reviewed by this or any other court.[13]

The Committee on Ministers' Powers made an exemplary effort to disentangle judicial, quasi-judicial, and administrative functions. It distinguished the jurisdiction of a minister from the slightly more independent

[12] See, for the British cases, R. v. Home Secretary [1917] 1 K. B. at p. 930; R. v. Leman Street Police Station Inspector, *ex parte* Venicoff [1920] 3 K. B. 73; and, for the American, Ng Fung Ho v. White (1922) 259 U. S. 276.

[13] Dormer v. Newcastle-upon-Tyne [1940] 2 K. B. at pp. 217–18.

jurisdiction of a ministerial tribunal. The quasi-judicial function, as contrasted with the judicial, is one in which the minister alone must be responsible because the question is one of policy. The committee would prefer that the facts be found by an independent tribunal and the decision on policy made by the minister. But, the administrators will protest, it is all one process.

The judicial element is sometimes elusive. In 1858 a Tasmanian Act referred disputes about lands to the Supreme Court whose decision was to be final. The statute directed the court to be guided by equity and good conscience only and by the best evidence that could be procured, although not such as would be required or admitted in ordinary cases; the court was not to be bound by the strict rules of law or equity in any case or by any technicalities or legal forms whatever. The court's action was held not to be a judicial action; its decisions could not be tested on appeal. Decisions could not be varied except by reference to some rule; the court here was free from all rules.[14] In another Australian case a statutory Board of Review for taxation matters was held not to be a court exercising judicial power. Lord Sankey's opinion contained the following passage:

> The authorities are clear to show that there are tribunals with many of the trappings of a court which nevertheless are not courts in the strict sense of exercising judicial power . . . A tribunal is not necessarily a court in this strict sense because it gives a final decision—nor because it hears witnesses on oath—nor because two or more contending parties appear before it between whom it has to decide—nor because

[14] Moses v. Parker [1891] A. C. 245.

it gives decisions which affect the rights of subjects—nor because there is an appeal to a court—nor because it is a body to which a matter is referred by another body.

In the opinion of the Privy Council this Tasmanian Board of Review, set up to deal with tax disputes, was an administrative and not a judicial tribunal.[15]

There has been one practical test whether an action is administrative or judicial, namely, the writ of certiorari. The London County Council, rashly believing that the Sunday Observance Acts could be deemed obsolete, proceeded through its Theatres Committee to issue licences for cinemas to open on Sunday. The licensing functions of justices of the peace (or of the bodies which have replaced them) have often been considered, particularly in respect of the issue of liquor licences. If they were administrative, certiorari would not lie; if they were judicial, certiorari would lie because it is an ancient prerogative writ drawn up for the purpose of enabling the court of King's Bench to control the action of inferior courts and to make it certain that they shall not exceed their jurisdiction. Here was the Theatres Committee exercising a non-existent jurisdiction; the Sunday Observance Acts being still in force, the committee could not license cinemas to be open on Sunday. The Court of Appeal refused to allow the London County Council to argue that the committee's action was an administrative act (and thus immune from review) and not a judicial act. The judges had no doubt that certiorari would issue against the committee.

15 Shell Co. of Australia v. Federal Commrs. of Taxation [1931] A. C. at pp. 296–97.

It is not necessary that it should be a court in the sense in which this court is a court; it is enough if it is exercising, after hearing evidence, judicial functions in the sense that it has to decide on evidence between a proposal and an opposition . . . if it is a tribunal which has to decide rights after hearing evidence and opposition, it is amenable to the writ of certiorari.[16]

So said Lord Justice Scrutton in an opinion which is sometimes criticized. His rather rough-and-ready test and Lord Sankey's negative symptoms show how difficult it is to draw the line. Thus the legislature sets its puzzles. For the citizen the main concern is his prospect of access to the law-courts if his rights are endangered by an administrative tribunal. The Committee on Ministers' Powers recommended that future legislation should allow anyone who is aggrieved by the decision of a minister or a ministerial tribunal to have an absolute right of appeal to the law-courts on any point of law but no right of appeal on any issue of fact. Then, qualifying its exclusion of appeal on points of fact, it added that the legislature might think certain types of legislation likely to create exceptional cases where some appeal on fact should be permitted; it had in mind in particular the war-pensions procedure evolved after the last war. Such appeal on fact, it suggested, should be to a tribunal consisting of a legal chairman (appointed by the Lord Chancellor) and two other persons. Some members of the committee, by the way, had plainly been perturbed by the idea of finality of fact-finding even in the holding of local inquiries; they feared that a government inspector, however complete

[16] R. v. London County Council [1931] 2 K. B. at p. 233.

his engineering experience, might by oversight mistake north for south or accept an engineering scheme where water was made to run uphill.

This separation of law and fact sounds attractively simple. It suggests such a division as has existed between the functions of judge and jury, though in England the diminishing use of juries (the result of a campaign for expediting the business of the courts, because a jury is a time-wasting institution) obscures the distinction. The administrative tribunal would find the facts and the courts would not interfere unless the absence of evidence or the perversity of the finding required them to intervene. The judges, who have the last word, can confidently draw the line between law and fact; for the rest of us it is not so easy. Marriage, for instance, seems at one time to be a question of fact in the courts, at another a question of law. A recent case in the English courts shows the kind of difficulty one encounters in distinguishing law from fact.[17] A town can acquire land compulsorily for housing, except when the land "forms part of any park, garden or pleasure ground or is otherwise required for the amenity or convenience of any house." The town of Ripon wanted twenty-three acres forming the grounds of a house named Highfield. The owners objected that the land was within the exception; a public inquiry followed; there was evidence that the land was let to a farmer for grazing; the Ministry of Health decided against the objectors. On appeal the judge said this was a question of fact; the Minister had made up his

[17] White and Collins v. Minister of Health [1939] 2 K. B. 838.

mind on proper materials and without misdirecting himself, and the court would not interfere. The owners went to the Court of Appeal where the Ministry argued that a court ought not to interfere with local housing authorities when carrying out their duties to house the people. The Court of Appeal proceeded to construe the statute. This was a matter of law; there had been a doubt whether the Ministry had not been inclined to take "or is otherwise required" as if it were "and is otherwise required." The Court of Appeal came to the conclusion that the land was part of a park. The jurisdiction to make an order depended on a finding of fact; if the land was park, the town had no jurisdiction to make the order for compulsory purchase and the Minister none to confirm it. Thus the Court of Appeal found a point of fact while deciding its point of law.

This persistent and awkward dilemma between administrative finality and judicial insistence upon private rights, this problem of "jurisdictional facts" and of "constitutional facts" is, of course, familiar to you. Mr. John Dickinson explained it in his *Administrative Justice and the Supremacy of Law* with a scholarship and a power of analysis which leave little more to be said. In the Ju Toy case, you remember, there was a decision by immigration authorities who had statutory power to exclude alien immigrants of Chinese nationality. They found that Ju Toy was born in China and was therefore within the statute. He said he was born in the United States. The Supreme Court held that the authorities' administrative finding was conclusive; it was a pure question of fact. On the other hand, if veterinary officials, acting for the public interest under statutory powers for eradicating animal diseases, kill a horse because it is diseased, their determination that the horse is diseased is not conclusive; a jury can find that the animal was not in fact diseased; the officials having acted in excess of their jurisdiction, the owner gets damages.

An important part of the complaint against administrative tribunals is that they adopt a procedure of their own. Sometimes the statute or regulation which creates the tribunal will exclude the legal profession from attending to represent parties, the object being presumably to save time and expense. Where two or three lawyers are gathered together, they will introduce their accustomed procedure, the opening speech, the examination in chief, cross-examination and re-examination of witnesses, and the occasional protests that something is not evidence, though the tribunals are not always bound by the strict laws of evidence. In England two well-known cases settled the right of the administrative agency to choose its own way of coming to a decision. One of these (*Board of Education v. Rice*) arose out of the statutory authority of the department to determine a dispute between the local education authority and the managers of a local school. The Lord Chancellor, Lord Loreburn, said that statutes were imposing on departments or officers of State the duty to decide questions "usually of a legislative kind." The questions sometimes involved law as well as fact; they might even involve law alone. The duty of the Board of Education was to ascertain the law and ascertain the facts. In doing so, they must act in good faith and listen to both sides, for that is a duty lying upon everyone who decides anything.[18] But they were not bound to treat such a question as though it were a trial. They could obtain information in any way they thought best, always giving a fair opportunity to those who were parties in the controversy for correcting or contradicting any relevant statement prejudicial to their view.

The other case, *R. v. Arlidge,* was more elaborate. A Housing Act told local authorities to make orders closing any dwelling-house unfit for human habitation. Notice of the closing order must be served on the owner; he had a right of appeal to the Local Government Board if he applied within fourteen days. The statute said that the procedure on such appeals should be such as the Board might by rules determine. On the appeal the Board could make such order as it thought equitable; the order would be binding and conclusive on all parties, subject to the right to go to the High Court on a question of law. The rules were to provide that the Board should not dismiss an appeal without holding a public local inquiry.

May I interrupt my story of the Arlidge case at this point in order to discuss the system of public local inquiries in England? They somewhat resemble coroners' inquests, which, while reaching a definite or indefinite finding of fact, perform the useful social function of ventilating local opinions and averting any impression that vital matters have been ignored or suppressed. These inquiries, held under different statutes, may vary from

18 [1911] A. C. 179.

small-scale meetings in the waiting room of a wayside railway station to full-dress assemblies in a big town hall with rows of barristers representing different interests. Here is an illustration from memory. An English city, having overflowed its ancient limits, desired to extend its boundaries so as to bring in the population which radiated from its centre and to organize its water supply and other public services on an enlarged scale. Under the relevant statute (since repealed) [19] notice of its proposals was published, and the local inquiry began. The presiding official, an inspector with engineering qualifications, briefly outlined the scope of the proceedings, and the leading counsel for the city made an opening speech and called municipal officials (the town clerk and the city treasurer, for instance) to substantiate his statements and submissions. These witnesses underwent prolonged cross-examination by counsel representing outside local authorities which were threatened with loss of territory. The general line of attack was the contention that the adjoining rural areas were content with the pastoral amenities which they at present enjoyed, and had no wish to be merged in a greater unit and be charged with higher local taxation to support its progressive expenditure. The outside bodies therefore sought to belittle the advantages of extension, to expose weaknesses in the city's administration, and to show that the proposals were unfair and unworkable. By the time these witnesses had been re-examined, the inquiry was fairly on its legs. In

[19] 51 & 52 Vict. c. 41, s. 54, restricted by 16 & 17 Geo. 5, c. 38, and replaced by 23 & 24 Geo. 5, c. 51, Part VI.

due course the advocates of the interests of the objectors had their say in turn and called their witnesses before a public audience which followed the proceedings closely. At length the inspector said one morning that the investigation had now lasted several days, that he thought he had gathered a proper appreciation of the points in issue, that he had other official appointments elsewhere in the near future, and that he suggested the proceedings might now be expedited so as to end in two days' time. The hint was taken, the inquiry was closed, the inspector departed; down went the curtain on the inquiry, and after many months the Ministry issued its decision. Nobody outside the department knew what the inspector had reported or how far his recommendations, if any, were reversed inside the department. One can understand, however, that the report would be circulated to different branches of the Ministry. What went on behind the scenes was team-work. If there were a point of law, the legal branch might have something to say; if there were a question of water supply or sewage disposal, it might need consideration by officials who had knowledge of the requirements and plans and activities of other adjoining cities or local bodies. The department must advise itself on several grounds because the extension of boundaries was a problem of local government. The city was a "county borough," the equivalent of a separate county in itself, a large hole punched in the map of the surrounding county. How far the big centres of population should be allowed to grow bigger still and thus to leave a mere residue of rural units with slender resources of local taxation—that was a matter of general policy which only the department could decide.

At these statutory inquiries the evidence is seldom taken on oath. Barristers are usually allowed to attend, but this depends on the statute or regulation governing the procedure. A shorthand note is sometimes taken. The inspector is experienced and sensible; if he were not, he would not be there. He is not specially equipped or qualified as a lawyer to deal with questions of evidence, but he has been given a common-sense code of general instructions telling him how he is to conduct the proceedings. Often the issue may be entirely technical—the efficiency of some engineering project. The proportion of justiciable issues in these inquiries is small. The inquiry is not the sole source of information. The inspector may have seen a file of correspondence before he goes down to the inquiry. He is sure to perambulate the scene to inform himself of the geographical and technical features. That may raise uncomfortable suspicions of his having received some amount of evidence *aliunde* without the interested persons having the chance to examine the witnesses.

The practising lawyer has his own views on this procedure. He asks that it be compared with true judicial process. Imagine, he says, that two people go to law; their dispute is referred to the law-courts; the law-courts send down a layman to hear the evidence; he takes unsworn testimony, comes back and writes a report to the judge which is not seen by the parties but is merely advisory; this report is circulated to several people at the law-courts who attach their remarks; an anonymous official ultimately delivers an impersonal judgment but gives no reasons. There is no unification of hearing and decision. How, asks the lawyer, can that be satisfactory?

The answer, perhaps rather a lame and apologetic answer, is that the comparison with the courts is misleading. Anyhow this latitude of procedure, this lapse from true judicial process, was the problem presented to the courts in the Arlidge case from which I broke off just now. Mr. Arlidge demanded to see the inspector's report to the department and to be heard thereafter again upon the whole case. The ultimate judicial tribunal, the House of Lords, so far from disapproving the procedure adopted by the department, regarded it as complying with all the essentials of justice and as having done complete justice to Mr. Arlidge. "Judicial methods," said Lord Shaw, "may, in many points of administration, be entirely unsuitable and produce delays, expense and public and private injury . . . Lawyerlike methods may find especial favour with lawyers. But that the judiciary should presume to impose its own methods on administrative or executive officers is a usurpation." [20]

This was a justification of departmental procedure which some lawyers and legal writers still regard as deplorable. Since the Rice and Arlidge cases were decided, a conception of "natural justice" has been developed; administrative tribunals are warned of certain minimum conditions of fair play upon which courts of law will insist. The Committee on Ministers' Powers expounded

[20] [1915] A. C. at p. 138.

them; a series of decisions under the Housing Acts has applied them.

To begin with, our law-courts have found themselves able to distinguish between the ministerial or administrative capacity of the official at one moment and his quasi-judicial capacity at another. If there were no objection by the property-owners, the Minister, making such inquiries as he thought necessary for informing himself whether it was in the public interest that he should make an order under the Housing Acts, would be acting in his ministerial or administrative capacity. As soon as objections were raised by persons interested, as soon as the value of the property of the objecting parties seemed to be threatened, he would be acting quasi-judicially. The Jarrow town council wanted a clearance order for demolishing all the houses in a specified area. The owners objected and said "if we pull down some and re-condition the others, we can make the area habitable and can reasonably comply with proper public health standards for the next fifteen or twenty years." This did not satisfy the town council. A government inspector came and held his inquiry. Afterwards the Minister, anxious to reconcile the conflicting views and to avoid the expense of the demolition programme, sent him back to Jarrow where he managed to persuade the city's medical officer of health and the property-owners to agree on a re-conditioning scheme. But the city still held out. It repudiated its medical officer, and it insisted on demolition. It passed resolutions to this effect and sent them up to the Ministry. Some correspondence ensued between the Ministry and the town clerk's office. The town clerk's letters contained fresh evidence in support of the view that mere reconditioning would not be enough; there was a fresh opinion from the medical officer, and another from the borough engineer who had not been a witness at the inquiry. It happened that a senior official in the housing branch of the Ministry was going to visit that part of the country. It was arranged for him and the inspector who held the inquiry to be in Jarrow on a certain day, where they met some city officials and discussed what could be done. The property-owners were not present. The Court of Appeal declared that the Ministry of Health, while acting in a quasi-judicial capacity, had done just what a quasi-judicial body cannot do. It had heard evidence from one side only, in the absence of the other side; it had viewed the property and formed its own opinion about it without giving the owners the chance to argue that the opinion it was inclined to form was such as could be readily met by means of repairs and alterations. The Ministry had listened to evidence given *ex parte,* evidence not given at the public inquiry. The Ministry's order was made upon improper materials and must be quashed. He had not exercised his powers in accordance with natural justice; he had failed to hear both sides; he had heard one side in the absence of the other.[21] There had been, in Lord Justice Maugham's words, an *ex parte* perambulation of the district. It was

> . . . of the highest possible importance that, where a quasi-judicial function is being exercised . . . as here, with the result of depriving people of their property, especially if it

---

[21] Lord Justice Greer, *in re* Errington and others [1935] 1 K. B. at p. 268.

is done without compensation, the persons concerned should be satisfied that nothing unfair has been done . . . and that *ex parte* statements have not been heard before the decision has been given, without any chance for the persons concerned to refute those statements.

Although, said Lord Justice Roche, it was sometimes said that the principles of natural justice were vague and difficult to ascertain, fortunately the principles of British justice had been authoritatively laid down; if judicial or quasi-judicial functions were to be exercised by a court or a board or any body of persons, it was necessary and essential to give a fair opportunity to those who are parties in the controversy to correct or to contradict any relevant statement prejudicial to their view. "In other words those principles of British justice proceed upon the basis that both sides have a right to be heard." [22]

Attempts were made to extend the decision in the Jarrow case. The Minister of Health had sent out a circular to local authorities saying that he was prepared to place the services of his staff at their disposal if there was any difficulty in preparing housing arrangements. An inspector was invited to Kingston-upon-Thames, and went round the district with the city's sanitary inspector. While looking at some houses, the Minister's inspector, trying to be helpful, said "that is the class of property which other local authorities are including in clearance orders." The house-owners sought to upset the subse-

[22] *Ibidem*, p. 281. There are, however, limits to the right of notice enjoyed by persons affected: see *ex parte* Death (1852) 18 Q. B. 647; R. v. Army Council (1917) 86 L. J. K. B., 1087; *ex parte* Venicoff [1920] 3 K. B. at p. 79.

quent clearance order on the ground that, in giving this advice, the Ministry did not approach the making of the order with an open mind. The court said that the statutes empowered the Ministry to do two things—to give advice and to consider quasi-judicially the confirmation of the order. When the inspector gave the advice it was an administrative and not a quasi-judicial act; nothing in the nature of a *lis* or lawsuit had yet been joined between the objecting property-owners and the town council; nothing unjudicial had been done.[23]

In a Birkenhead case the town clerk had approached the Ministry for advice about a clearance order before the local inquiry was in prospect. The court held that this was unobjectionable. At that early stage, before objection was made, the Minister was not acting judicially.[24] Then in a Sunderland case, after a public local inquiry was over, the city sent a deputation up to London to see the Ministry. This was the converse of the Jarrow case where the Minister had sent someone down from London to see the local officials on the spot. The Sunderland deputation said that it did not discuss with the Ministry the housing on the site to which the inquiry had related. The property-owner said it was natural for him to suppose that his site had been mentioned without his being present. It was not enough for justice to be done; it must manifestly appear to be done. The judge said that any reasonable person might have come to the conclusion that the deputation did discuss the site to which the inquiry had related. The court therefore quashed the or-

[23] *In re* Offer [1936] 1 K. B. 40.

[24] *In re* Frost [1935] 1 K. B. 286.

der. But afterwards the Court of Appeal accepted evidence that the site had never been mentioned at the interviews. If so, no harm had been done; the order was therefore restored.[25] Then there was a rather fanciful case where a town wanted a compulsory purchase order for the site of an aerodrome. During the inquiry the inspector flew over the site in an aeroplane piloted by a witness for the promoters; it was objected that there was nobody present in the aeroplane to represent the site-owners. That objection was overruled.[26]

Natural justice amounts to this. In the first place there must be no bias. The effect of a pecuniary interest needs no emphasis. In the English case of *Dimes v. Grand Junction Canal*[27] a decree of the Lord Chancellor himself was set aside because he was interested as shareholder to the amount of several thousand pounds in the company which was being granted relief. Nobody supposed that Lord Chancellor Cottenham's decision would be influenced by this interest, but it was an opportunity to set an example. If there is a possibility of bias from kindred or any other cause, the judge ought not to sit.[28] Our English cases stipulate that the bias must be a real bias in favour of one of the parties. There was once an attempt to prevent a mayor from adjudicating on a charge of cruelty to a horse on the ground that, being a subscriber to the Royal Society for the Prevention of Cruelty to Ani-

25 Horn v. Minister of Health [1937] 1 K. B. 164.

26 *In re* Manchester (Ringway Airport) Compulsory Purchase Order, (1935) 153 Law Times, p. 219.

27 (1852) 3 H. L. C. 759.

28 R. v. Rand (1866) L. R. 1 Q. B. 230.

mals, he would be biased against the defendant.[29] Another time someone said that the chairman of the local magistrates ought not to try a charge against a motorist of exceeding the speed limit, because he had once remarked that it would be a good thing if the motor industry were destroyed. The judge observed that a magistrate was at liberty to entertain strong views on a subject, though it were better if he kept his views to himself.[30] But now the Committee on Ministers' Powers has discovered a new kind of bias, namely, the interest that an enthusiastic minister might have in his official work, where his department might be approaching a decision with a desire that it should go one way rather than the other. You may think that this is setting the Minister an exacting standard; he has a duty to promote some public service such as housing or health or transport and yet at the critical moment he must hold himself back. Is not the departmental interest also the public interest?

The rule against bias is expressed in the maxim that no one must be a judge in his own cause. So long as the idea survived in England that courts had power to overrule statutes, the usual instance of the sort of statute which might properly be declared void was one which infringed this maxim.[31] We have already noticed an English case where the Postmaster-General was not prevented from being judge in his own cause in a dispute with a tele-

[29] R. v. Mayor and Justices of Deal (1881) 45 L. T. 439.

[30] R. v. Worthing Justices *ex parte* Wilder (1902) 73 J. P. 76.

[31] See Sir F. Pollock's interesting excursus in the chapter on "Sovereignty in English Law" in his *First Book of Jurisprudence.*

phone subscriber.[32] Other instances occur in the British statute-book. A Restriction of Ribbon Development Act was passed to control building along the sides of our roads; it gives the Minister of Transport jurisdiction in disputes between local highway authorities and land-owners. But the Trunk Roads Act has made the Minister himself a highway authority in respect of the big arterial routes.[33] Nor does the resultant position seem to have been accidental.

The second broad rule of natural justice is that no party is to be condemned unheard; if his right to be heard is to be worth having, he must know in good time the case he has to meet. The Jarrow housing case, mentioned just now, is a good illustration. An earlier one is given by an eighteenth-century judge who pointed out that God did not remove Adam from Eden without first calling upon him to make his defence.[34] In the opinion of the Committee on Ministers' Powers there is probably a third rule of natural justice, which entitles the party to know the reason for the decision, be it judicial or quasi-judicial, and possibly a fourth principle, namely, that when statutes prescribe an oral hearing before a Minister's inspector as a means of informing the Minister's mind before some ministerial decision, the inspector's report should be available for the parties to see. Reasons ought,

[32] See p. 52, above.

[33] See 25 & 26 Geo. 5, c. 47, and 1 Edw. 8 & 1 Geo. 6, c. 5, s. 1. For other instances see 15 & 16 Vict. c. 63, ss. 19, 20 (Valuation Commissioner in Ireland), 1 Edw. 7, c. 22, s. 80 (the Factory and Workshop Act, now repealed), and 6 Edw. 7, c. 37, s. 6 (possible appeal to Local Government Board for Ireland from its inspector's order).

[34] (1724) 1 Strange 567 (Bentley's case). And see preamble to 4 Hen. 8, c. 8 ("contrary to all laws, right reason and good conscience").

of course, to be given for legal decisions. Otherwise students cannot learn the law, practitioners cannot find arguments, parties cannot feel that their cases have had serious attention, and courts of appeal have nothing to upset or confirm. Perhaps it does not necessarily follow that non-judicial tribunals must give reasons. The grant or refusal of a licence need not be made the occasion for a full-dress statement of policy by the licensing body. On an appeal by a man who was aggrieved that he had been declared ineligible for readmission to the London Stock Exchange without reason given, the court said that the Stock Exchange Committee need not give reasons.[35] In small matters even judicial tribunals refrain; the magistrate may just say "Case dismissed" or "Pay five shillings." The Committee on Ministers' Powers thought that reasons should always be given by administrative tribunals, especially where a Minister modifies the recommendations or rejects the findings of fact in the inspector's report. It saw presumably no danger that policy might lose its elasticity under the pressure of volumes of departmental decisions. As for publishing the inspector's report itself, the committee favoured it, although in the Arlidge case Lord Haldane said that the report, being intended solely for the Minister's information, was rightly kept private. Ministers have declined to furnish copies of these reports for this reason.[36] Some critics think that publication will shift the responsibility for decision from the Minister to the inspector, that the inspector's findings

35 Cassel v. Inglis [1916] 2 Ch. 211.

36 See Denby (William) & Son v. Min. of Health [1936] 1 K. B. 337.

will tend to be conclusive, and that he may be tempted to make his report colourless and valueless where at present he makes it a frank and confidential and therefore an informative document. Publication both of a Minister's reasons [37] and of an inspector's report [38] is occasionally prescribed by statute.

What I have been saying has, I fear, been too general or too insular to be helpful. I have spoken of some of these matters as being *sub judice*. They have political aspects; yet it would be a pity if they were approached solely by way of political avenues. Nobody would easily find in the British statute-book anything to show which party was in power when an enactment has created administrative jurisdiction. Equally it would be a pity if these developments were written off as foreign and unnatural—rather as Dicey in his Oxford lectures wrote off administrative law as something alien and continental. We may as well accept them as indigenous and recognize that they have grown up with no sinister design of destroying liberty, but with a sincere desire to do the State some service. There are instances where, almost to our surprise, an administrative tribunal works well and is popular—the Board of Tax Appeals in the United States, independent and judicial, or the Special Commissioners of Income Tax in Britain, impartial although Crown

[37] See the Restriction of Ribbon Development Act, 25 & 26 Geo. 5, c. 47, s. 7(4) (Minister to publish summary of facts as found by him and of his reasons for the decision).

[38] See 11 & 12 Geo. 5, c. 51, sch. 5 (inquiry by impartial person appointed by the Board of Education who must not be a government employee).

servants appointed by the Treasury. Can study reveal any reasons for their success?

We shall agree that we cannot do without judicial review; the courts are the only protectors of our rights; it is their function to protect us. Yet if every administrative tribunal's decisions are to be reviewed, we might as well abolish the tribunals; if we did, we should swamp the courts with work for which they have neither time nor aptitude. We have been saying for years that what is wanted is more of the judicial element in the tribunals and more sympathy and understanding of the administrative element in the law-courts. If the giving of reasons for decisions will make the tribunals more careful, let us insist on it. If the whole question is one of personnel, let us insist on having the right persons. How far is there a genuine complaint that the parties cannot feel quite the same confidence in the competence and integrity of an impersonal department as they do in the judge whom they see and hear in a law-court?

The history books have told us all about the Court of Star Chamber, "a court of politicians enforcing a policy, not a court of judges enforcing the law." [39] It was not so bad a court in its day; it was needed because other courts did not properly enforce the law. The Star Chamber Abolition Act expressly brought us back to Magna Carta and "due process of law"; it insisted on trial "in the ordinary courts of justice and by the ordinary course of the law." [40]

[39] F. W. Maitland, *Constitutional Law*, p. 263.
[40] 16 Car. 1, c. 10.

Professor Holdsworth has written that it is largely through the abolition of the Star Chamber that English law knows a theory of ministerial responsibility and not a system of administrative law.[41] Professor Maitland saw another aspect. Speaking of the continuity of the old law of England, he observed that the medieval criminal law could be preserved because a Court of Star Chamber would supply its deficiencies; the old private law could be preserved because the Court of Chancery was composing an appendix to it; trial by jury could be preserved, developed, and transfigured because other modes of trial were limiting it to an appropriate sphere.

> The Star Chamber and the Chancery were dangerous to our political liberties. Bacon could tell King James that the Chancery was the court of his absolute power. But, if we look abroad, we shall find good reason for thinking that, but for these institutions, our old-fashioned national law, unable out of its own resources to meet the requirements of a new age, would have utterly broken down, and the 'ungodly jumble' would have made way for Roman jurisprudence and for despotism. Were we to say that equity saved the common law, and that the Court of Star Chamber saved the constitution, even in this paradox there would be some truth.[42]

Will the historian some day go further and say that our old-fashioned national law, unable out of its own resources to meet the requirements of a new age, has been preserved because it was supplemented by a system, however unsystematic, of administrative tribunals?

[41] *History of English Law,* I, 516; see also IV, 59, 106.
[42] *Social England,* edited by F. D. Traill, II, 489.

5. The Written Laws

Where the laws be few, they leave much to arbitrary power; but where they be many, they leave more.—
HARRINGTON: OCEANA

A FAMOUS British draftsman, the late Sir Mackenzie Chalmers, had a favourite story with a Benthamite moral. In his enthusiasm for the improvement of the statute-book, he was once urging a high official to agree to the orderly re-writing of a long and untidy series of statutes dealing with the sale of food and drugs. "Why trouble about that?" was the reply; "we know all about the law inside the department and the public finds out in the police-court." That probably apocryphal tale illustrates an aspect of administrative law which it may be worth while to examine. Here is an ever-increasing coil of legislation, direct and indirect, winding itself round the citizen. Are we satisfied with the standard of his knowledge of it or of his interest in it? Are we satisfied with his exposure to laws so complicated and so copiously amended that only experts can understand them? Is there not a tendency for experts of all kinds to monopolize the mysteries of their special subject and to take away the key of knowledge?

These are problems partly of publicity and partly of form. First, then, of publicity, without which the most willing citizen can neither understand nor obey. The common-law countries have built up their administration of criminal justice on the principle that no court can allow anyone to plead that he did not know his action was wrong. But we must not think of law only in terms of crimes and penalties. With the larger use of legislation as an instrument for national welfare, for neighbourliness, and for the application of scientific discovery, we have a stronger and more social interest to have the laws known and obeyed. Suppose there is an outbreak of cattle disease in England and laws have been passed for stamping it out by restricting the movement of cattle in affected areas; it is not enough to publish the stand-still orders in the *London Gazette* or in the official Statutory Rules and Orders series. A prime minister once wistfully confessed in the House of Commons that the *Gazette* was one of the few publications he did not read. Certainly farmers do not study these official sources. An Act of 1746, enabling rules to be made for preventing the spread of distemper among horned cattle, directed that the rules be read in church after prayers on the following Sunday and monthly in the future.[1] Nowadays we must send a policeman or other official to every farm, near and far, to notify the orders and ensure general co-operation. The administration must use all possible machinery of communication, the newspapers and the wireless broadcast. It has been suggested in England that the newspapers should be compelled to publish official announcements. What is the use when the public cannot be compelled to read them? The United States published an *Official*

[1] 19 Geo. 2, c. 5.

Bulletin in the last war, and public-spirited efforts were made in the nineteen-thirties with the *United States Daily* to persuade citizens to take an interest in public matters affecting them. Normally the newspapers collaborate in reproducing or summarizing paragraphs officially supplied. Journalists may be trusted to pick out any feature which may interest or amuse. But a newspaper summary has been known to be incomplete or even inaccurate. As with printing, so with broadcasting. The citizen neither reads nor listens with the law-conscious mind. Something is half-read or half-heard, and the next stage is another official communication beginning with the formula "Some misunderstanding appears to have arisen over the recent announcement" about this or that, or perhaps even a prosecution.

Last summer in Britain somebody suggested in a newspaper that the ringing of church bells might be used as a signal to indicate the advent of invaders. A parson subsequently on June 16 rang his bell for morning service on Sunday; a policeman took action in the belief that this was an offence. Three days later a Control of Noise Order was issued, which for the first time specifically forbade the ringing of church bells except as a military warning. Three weeks afterwards the magistrates dealt with the parson's case; they convicted him and sentenced him to imprisonment. After some days of detention he was released, and eventually he appealed successfully against his conviction and sentence. It was clear that the order of June 19, which the magistrates had purported to be enforcing, had not been made at the date of the alleged offence and indeed that the magistrates had never seen the order at all.

I fancy I have already asked the rhetorical question whether we are all obliged to read the newspapers or to listen to the wireless?[2] Last July the Minister of Food made a Tea (Rationing) Order. It was made on the ninth; official prints were not available till the eleventh. A grocer was summoned for having sold unrationed tea on the morning of the ninth. The new order had been mentioned in a wireless announcement on the night of the eighth, publicity being deliberately delayed to prevent the public from laying in stocks. The grocer admitted listening to the wireless news on the night before (though I do not know why he should have been forced to admit it), but said he had not appreciated that rationing was to be introduced next day. The magistrate believed him and refused to punish him beyond making him pay the costs. It was not, said the magistrate, a satisfactory way of publishing a law; people "listening in" did not pay the same rapt attention as they would when consciously studying an official document. On the eve of the present war the Home Secretary made a Lighting (Restriction) Order which, amongst other things, obliged a cyclist to carry a red rear lamp. Three days later, before official prints of the order were available, a cyclist was run over by a motor-car. When he afterwards sued the driver for dam-

[2] In 1923 a German law for the publication of ordinances, printed in the Reichsgesetzblatt of that year, Part I, p. 959, provided for broadcasting. I owe this reference to Prof. Karl Loewenstein of Amherst College.

ages for negligence, the driver said it was wrong of the cyclist not to have displayed the red lamp as prescribed by the order. The judge held that the cyclist was not at fault in failing to comply with an order of which he could not have known.

The rule about the operation of a statute in Britain is clear. A statute does not derive its force from promulgation. The Clerk of the Parliaments has to indorse on each new Act the date when it receives the royal assent; if nothing has been prescribed to the contrary, the statute takes effect upon that day,[3] and, since the law takes no account of parts of a day, at the very first moment when that day begins. By an engaging legal fiction all citizens are vicariously present in the persons of their elected representatives when a statute is made; so they know all about it. But there is no such publicity about delegated legislation. During the last war the Food Controller made an order requisitioning peas and beans. The order was made on a Tuesday; a purchase of beans was carried through on that day; neither the parties nor the public knew or could have known of the order till next morning, when there was a notice in the newspapers. Was the purchase affected by the order? The court refused to follow the analogy of a statute and to say that the order took effect from the beginning of the Tuesday on which it was made. Orders, observed the judge, had not the publicity of a statute; many such orders, to be effective at all, must not be known till they were published. He held that the

[3] 33 Geo. 3, c. 13; see also 52 & 53 Vict. c. 63, s. 36(2), and Tomlinson v. Bullock (1878) 4 Q. B. D. 232.

order did not operate till it was known next morning.[4] The decision has been criticized. If statutes or deeds take effect from the beginning of the day on which they are made, why not the delegated legislation also? As we have previously seen, Congress has successfully related the operation of executive orders to the date when they are filed for official publication. It is a prudent precaution against the occasional short-sightedness of officials who think it adroit to keep orders up their sleeves. Even with the best intentions in Britain there can be an unfortunate hiatus between operation and publicity. We still have to "find out in the police-court." Anxious citizens should erect propitiatory altars to the Unknown Law.

Let me turn from the accessibility to the intelligibility of legislation, original or delegated. Whether law comes down from above or up from below, whether law is obeyed from fear of penalties or because it is the public consciousness of what is orderly and right, the legislative ideal is a simple, concise, self-explanatory code. Alas! that ideal is only to be found in the ideal commonwealth. In Utopia, says More, they have but few laws.

> They very much condemn other nations whose laws, together with the commentaries on them, swell up so many volumes; for they think it an unreasonable thing to oblige men to obey a body of laws that are both of such a bulk and so dark as not to be read and understood by everyone of the subjects.

[4] Johnson v. Sargant [1918] 1 K. B. 101. In Jones v. Robson [1901] 1 Q. B. at p. 680, the court thought that the Home Secretary's order (prohibiting the use of an explosive) took effect when made; the question was whether compliance with statutory requirements about notice was a condition precedent; the words were held "merely directory."

Well, that was Utopia. Gulliver's travels took him to a country where no law was allowed to exceed in words the number of letters in the national alphabet, namely, twenty-two.

> But indeed few of them extend even to that length. They are expressed in the most plain and simple terms, wherein those people are not mercurial enough to discover above one interpretation.

In the world of fact statutes are many, long, and obscure. Their study is for the most part confined to professional and sometimes mercurial readers. The literary appeal is inconspicuous. In one of his letters Napoleon says he thinks little of a government whose edicts are always literary compositions. Draftsmanship has to omit frills. Lord Blackburn complained of the draftsman's tendency to keep changing the form of words when change of meaning was not intended, just to improve the graces of the style and to avoid using the same words twice.[5] On the whole, the layman studies legislation vicariously. He asks his lawyer what it is all about. If he cannot afford so much, there may be voluntary agencies which will help him. In Britain there are citizens' information bureaus, and the legal profession is developing a scheme of legal aid to poor persons, which, though not yet as generous as the services given by the medical profession, is well worth while. Administrative law often means to the layman the filling up of blank forms which are intricate as well as intrusive. The task may seem easy,

[5] Hadley v. Perks, L. R. 1 Q. B. 437.

but many people are glad of help. A few laymen have attempted the study of statutes. "Up betimes," wrote Samuel Pepys in his diary, "and to my office, and there read all the morning in my statute-book." He happened to have a special interest in a special problem. The young Abraham Lincoln passed swiftly from Aesop's *Fables* and *Robinson Crusoe* to the *Laws of Indiana* and the *Revised Statutes of Illinois*. The law and the legislature were his destination. Is there anything we can do for lesser folk, to interest and instruct them? Ought we to try harder to teach the law to the young? In the time of Elizabeth, Martin Bucer, a learned Cambridge professor whose name recalls some of the writings of John Milton, had the fancy that the civil laws might be commodiously reduced to brief summaries in verse, to be learnt in youth rather like nursery rhymes and chanted by everybody in later life.[6] Metre may assist memory, but we have yet to see our poets versify even the simple paragraphs of Magna Carta. Jeremy Bentham, always laudably anxious that the law should be "notorious to all," drew up a portentous Inaugural Declaration to be made by legislators. They were to undertake to make and keep those parts of the law in which all persons have an immediate interest "in such a state as they may without difficulty form the matter of the earliest instruction administered in schools." All this, I fear, is just the speculation of academic optimists. At least, however, we can focus attention on the improvement of form. We need not make the riddle harder.

[6] *Scripta Anglicana, De Regno Christi*, II, c. lvi (*de civilium legum repurgatione et explicatione*).

In some sensible rules which Montesquieu laid down for legislative expression he includes the advice that laws should not shock the nature of things, because that is one of the ways of bringing law into disrepute. Law cannot afford to look silly. It is hard not to smile at a passage in a twentieth-century statute passed at Westminster about mental deficiency. A person may be dealt with in a particular way

"if, in addition to being a defective, he is a person . . . who is in receipt of poor relief at the time of giving birth to an illegitimate child." [7]

It makes sense legally because (by virtue of the Interpretation Act) words importing the masculine gender shall include females, so that "he" includes "she." [8] It is good drafting and bad biology. Ludicrous passages in the statute-book may be due either to sheer oversight or to obsolescence. Sir Courtenay Ilbert gave you some examples of mistakes in his Carpentier lectures in 1913.[9] Most people's favourite is the Act of George III under which the penalties are to go half to the informer and half to the poor of the parish; the only penalty imposed by the Act is transportation for fourteen years.[10] Here are other oddities. An Act of 1694 imposing duties on marriages, births, and deaths and on bachelors and widowers to finance the war against France has the words "for and upon the birth of every person or child, the sum of five shillings." [11] The London Brighton and South Coast Rail-

[7] 3 & 4 Geo. 5, c. 28, s. 2 (1) (*b*); *cf.* c. 38, s. 3 (1) (*c*).
[8] 52 & 53 Vict. c. 63, s. 1 (1) (*a*).
[9] *Mechanics of Law Making*, p. 101.
[10] 52 Geo. 3, c. 146.
[11] 6 & 7 Will. & Mar. c. 6, s. 3.

way Act of 1846 prescribed that the half-yearly meetings of the company should be held on the thirty-first day of July and the thirty-first day of February.[12] Anybody who has often to consult the statute-book is sure to have noticed the inevitable minor instances of oversight. The Conveyancing and Law of Property Act, 1881, contained in Part I of its first schedule a list of statutes headed "Acts Affected": there is nothing in the text of the Act to hang this list upon.[13] The Artisans' and Labourers' Dwellings Act, 1879, mentions mortgages which are to be "in the form set forth in the third schedule hereto"; there is no such schedule.[14] The Public Libraries Act, 1901, is intituled "an Act to amend the Acts relating to public libraries, museums and gymnasiums and to regulate the liability of managers of libraries to proceedings for libel"; there is nothing about libel in the statute.[15] This kind of accident, due to failure to check the Bill in its final condition, is not uncommon.[16] There are cases too where a marginal note has not been altered to conform with the amendment of a clause in a Bill,[17] or where references to numbered sections have not been adjusted to subsequent

[12] 9 & 10 Vict. c. cclxxxiii: see 17 & 18 Vict. c. lxi.

[13] 44 & 45 Vict. c. 41: see 45 & 46 Vict. c. 39, s. 2 (1).

[14] 42 & 43 Vict. c. 64: see 43 Vict. c. 8.

[15] 1 Edw. 7, c. 19.

[16] See also 32 & 33 Vict. c. 19, s. 42, referring to 6 & 7 Vict. c. 106, when it means 6 & 7 Will. 4: see 22 & 23 Geo. 5, c. 46, s. 31 (4) "last succeeding subsection of this Act" instead of "last preceding . . ." And see 49 Geo. III, cc. 32 and 110 (tax of 1s. on official salaries &c., which was meant to be 1s. in every 20s.), and 5 & 6 Will. 4, c. 34, s. 1 (omission of "not").

[17] See 4 Edw. 7, c. 9, s. 11, "Decision of court final," where on the contrary the section gives a right of appeal, and 7 & 8 Geo. 5, c. 5, s. 2, where the marginal note mentions an Order in Council instead of an order of the Board of Trade.

re-numbering. In a rather controversial Bill in 1931 the first clause mentioned the Minister of a particular department, adding the convenient words "hereinafter referred to as 'the Minister.'" Unfortunately the House of Lords threw out this first clause, so that, as the Act now stands, the abbreviation "the Minister" is used throughout with no key to tell us which minister is intended, though of course we can guess.[18]

Perhaps one should add to this category of misadventures the difficulties which can arise in statutes, as on tombstones, through omitted or misplaced punctuation. The judges in England can ignore punctuation in interpreting statutes.[19] Draftsmen are trained not to rely upon punctuation. Bills often omit commas and semicolons; these are sometimes inserted for the convenience of readers when Bills become Acts, though not in the case of local Acts. We have a legend in England that there was once a Tariff Act of the United States which said that all foreign fruit-plants should be free from duty. The hyphenated word "fruit-plants" being printed "fruit, plants," foreign bananas, oranges, and lemons had to be admitted duty-free until the mistake was corrected by an amending Act. Akin to this class of case is a cheerful instance once mentioned to me by a learned friend in Michigan University who kept a museum of statutory freaks:

> No one shall carry any dangerous weapon upon the public highway except for the purpose of killing a noxious animal or a policeman in the execution of his duty.

---

[18] 21 & 22 Geo. 5, c. 42.

[19] But see 26 Geo. 5 & 1 Edw. 8, c. 1, sch. 1, Part II, for an unusual instance of the adjusting of commas and semicolons by statute.

The judges, I daresay, could have construed that clause as the legislature intended. In their benevolence they have occasionally interpreted the draftsman's language so as to make sense rather than nonsense.[20] But, being human, they do not always resist the temptation to tell the draftsman what they think of him and his ways. Perhaps they do so with the more vigour because of a kind of instinctive dislike which they have sometimes seemed to exhibit towards statute law. Coke and Mansfield, you remember, talked as though the common law must be greater than any Act of Parliament. The balance between common law and statute law has been more and more disturbed by the weight of legislation whereby alone certain social developments can be introduced. Broadly, I suppose, case law deals with the isolated point and with the past; as Bentham viciously observed, the judges make the law as a man trains his dog, by waiting till the dog has done something wrong and then beating him. Statutes are more universal and deal with the future. I am wandering rather far from administrative law, but, since so much of it is statute law, I do suggest that statute law is as good a kind of law as any other. When Boswell thought of entering the legal profession, a friend told him that it was one in which any plodding blockhead could excel. Dr. Johnson, to whom Boswell repeated the remark, made one of his sledge-hammer comments:

Why, Sir, in the *formulary and statutory* part of law a plodding blockhead may excel; but in the *ingenious and rational* part of law a plodding blockhead never can excel.

[20] See Salmon v. Duncombe (1886) 11 App. Cas. 627.

The moral of that is that any fool can deal with statutes. Well, against Johnson let me cite another famous figure in English literature. Macaulay went out to India in 1834 to work on legislative drafting. His previous success in the law can be measured by the solitary guinea he had once earned for prosecuting someone for stealing poultry. He wrote home enthusiastically of his new work. It was as fine an employment of the intellect as anyone could conceive. "I ought to tell you," he added, "that the more progress I make as a legislator, the more intense my contempt for the mere technical study of law becomes." Macaulay drafted what after many years of revision by other hands became the famous Indian penal code; this, according to Sir James Stephen, is simpler and better expressed than Livingston's code for Louisiana. Stephen calls Macaulay's work "concise and even beautiful." A modern exponent has claimed that legislative drafting is a high and splendid branch of the art of using language,[21] an agonizing creative effort, an expert technique which only the instructed reader can appreciate. Those who have a close-up view of the work of legislative draftsmen soon feel towards them a veneration which hardly stops short of idolatry; but for the moment I am thinking rather of the uninstructed readers. It would not, I believe, be unfair to say that the laws enacted in the legislature at Westminster are so fashioned as to be proof against destructive criticism in the House of Commons and against destructive interpretation in the law-courts. The smallest possible target must be offered for discussion

[21] See Sir Alison Russell, *Legislative Drafting and Forms*, 4th ed., p. 12.

and amendment. The natural order of the clauses must be perverted because of the paramount requirement that the Bill shall be passed; technical rules of judicial interpretation and a mysteriously algebraic vocabulary will be relied upon in order to economize words. There is an inevitable risk that administrators may forget the limitations of the lay mind. A statute enacted at Westminster, for instance, may talk about England and Scotland. Somebody will wonder about Wales. He may not know that, in a statute passed in the reign of George II dealing with the window-tax, there is an unobtrusive section which says that expressions relating to England shall be construed as referring also to Wales and the town of Berwick-upon-Tweed.[22] One cannot blame the draftsman for taking advantage of that compression: the rest of us ought to know it by now. But here is a worse puzzle. During the present war the postal charges in Britain have been increased, the telephone charges were correspondingly raised, and legislation was needed to adapt the contracts of telephone subscribers. Everybody knows the difference between a telegram and a telephone; you read the one and listen to the other. The statute which was passed never mentions the word "telephone," but uses the words "telegraph contracts" which would not attract the notice of the telephone subscriber. The Post Office employs this bit of algebra because it knows that the law-courts decided sixty years ago in *Attorney General v. Edison Telephone Co.* that "telegraph" includes telephone.[23] This is good drafting and judge-proof; it is not fool-proof.

[22] 20 Geo. II, c. 42, s. 3.

[23] (1881) 6 Q. B. D.

Now there are some provisions which it is just impossible to express in simple language. The fault, as Aristotle said, is not in the draftsman, but in the nature of the thing. A body of experts was set up in 1927 to clarify and re-write the distressing series of statutes which contain the British law of income tax. Many years later it published a report and a draft Bill. The report remarked that the ordinary layman, conscious of the simplicity of his own exiguous salary, complained of the complication of the law. If, said the committee disarmingly, he expects that the result of our labours will be to satisfy his aspirations for a short and simple code, he is doomed to grievous disappointment. The fate of the draft Bill is instructive. Framed in an agreed form, it was subjected to intensive study which has gone on so long that already the accumulated amendments contained in several subsequent Finance Acts would make it essential now to redraft the Bill entirely.

If in this connection I repeat yet again that the delegated legislation often concerns ordinary men and women even more intimately than the parent statute, you will have guessed why. The statute has to be drafted in a compressed and technical form so as to be as far as possible Parliament-proof. The delegated legislation is under no such necessity. It is not going to be wrangled over word by word and line by line and clause by clause. It can be framed with full regard for the people who have to obey it, the wayfaring men who may err therein. Its lay-out can be in logical sequence; if desired, it can use six lines for what a statute might try to squeeze into only one. If it be right to say with Horace *brevis esse laboro, obscurus fio,* the delegated legislation need run no risk of obscurity. And so it sometimes happens that rules, regulations, and orders composed by an administrator who is not a trained draftsman may be more easy for the average citizen to understand. But then the untrained draftsman may not appreciate the technical aspects of *ultra vires.* The Committee on Ministers' Powers, anxious to preserve judicial scrutiny and to avert illegality, pressed that delegated legislation should be framed by trained draftsmen. Peradventure, it said, there might be ten cases of *ultra vires* rules and orders; if the use of the expert's services would eliminate nine of them, it would be an important gain. In London the delegated legislation is, in the more awkward cases, undertaken by the official experts who have drafted the Acts; in routine cases it is done by the legal advisers of the departments concerned. It is well drafted; but good drafting in the technical sense is not necessarily clear drafting in the popular sense. The Committee on Ministers' Powers, by the way, suggested that explanatory notes might usefully be appended to delegated legislation to explain changes in the law.

When Sir Courtenay Ilbert lectured to you, he told you something of the Statute Law Committee of which he was chairman. It is an unpaid body of experts in drafting and in administration. Within its modest range it works disinterestedly to make the written law of Britain more accessible, to have it adequately indexed, and to promote the improvement of form. Ilbert touched upon three processes employed for those purposes.

The first is the humdrum, unambitious process of statute law revision—expurgation of what is dead and official republication of the residue which is still alive. Quantities of statutes are expressly repealed in the ordinary course of legislation but there is plenty of obsolete and impliedly repealed matter left. Under English law no statute ceases to operate merely through disuse. In 1903 a Welsh chimney-sweep had a family quarrel, went out into the street, and fired a revolver in the direction of his brother's window. Somebody remembered that the Statute of Northampton, enacted in the second year of Edward III, makes it an offence for any man, great or small, to go or ride armed by night or by day. That was good enough. The chimney-sweep was indicted under that statute at assizes and was convicted.[24] His counsel protested against the resurrection of so mouldy an anachronism. The judge said in effect "Not at all; we can't have people firing revolvers in streets." So, you see, a pre-gunpowder statute still serves for a post-gunpowder offence. We like our statutes old. Nothing is dead, however long forgotten, unless Parliament says so. Consequently, before we can have a new official edition of Revised Statutes, we have a Statute Law Revision Act which lists a mass of dead statutes, sections, or words and formally repeals them. Under this process one hundred and sixteen volumes of Acts were reduced to eighteen by

[24] See E. Stewart Fay, *Hanged by a Comma*, 1937, p. 15.

this expurgating process in the eighteen-sixties. A second edition was at once put in hand. If it were not for the war, we should be starting a third edition now. There are certain drawbacks in statute law revision. It is not safe to include any controversial item; Sunday Observance Acts had better not be touched; let sleeping dogs lie. One can only cut out; one cannot improve or amend. One may have to preserve the ridiculous. The Profane Oaths Act, 1745, has the following penalties for swearing:

for a day-labourer, common soldier or common seaman,	one shilling
for everybody else under the degree of a gentleman	two shillings
for gentlemen and upwards	five shillings

Once convicted, you are, as the bridge players say, vulnerable; the penalty is doubled next time. That class-conscious tariff looks obsolete; but the statute still appears in textbooks; apparently it is not yet dead enough to be repealed.

The second method of improvement is consolidation. Where there is a series of statutes on any subject, they are replaced by a single orderly statute. This is an old remedy. Bacon recommended it to James I. Samuel Pepys discussed it with William Prynne and wrote in his diary "if it were done, it would be a short work to know the law, which appears a very noble good thing." An early example is the Elizabethan Statute of Labourers. The process was not uncommon in the eighteen-twenties, a period which we are sometimes told to regard as exhibiting the lowest depths of bad draftsmanship. What is modern about consolidation in Britain is the device of remitting Bills of this kind to a Joint Select Committee of both Houses of Parliament for quiet examination. The draftsman attends and explains that the new neat clauses do no more than reproduce the old untidy law; on that understanding, Parliament gives the Bill an easy passage. If any amendment were introduced, the atmosphere would be changed; any member of Parliament could then propose other amendments of his own, and the Bill might be smothered to death. In the last few years, however, some vast consolidations of local government and public health enactments have been successfully achieved in spite of the presence of amendments. The amendments were non-controversial, being merely designed to modernize and standardize the old law. The proposals were first scrutinized by a very strong committee of experts, whose recommendations were accepted. Members of Parliament were good enough to forego their power of amendment. Consolidation may be unpopular with root-and-branch reformers because it reproduces and perpetuates laws which they dislike. On the other hand, the more clearly the law is re-written, the easier it is to amend. Indeed the consolidation of poor-law enactments in 1927 was undertaken because it was desired to amend the law by the Local Government Act in 1929; the enactments were too tangled to amend without first re-writing them. The process of re-writing is not as easy as it looks; it is not just scissors-and-paste work; it is good training in draftsmanship. Coke said, "For digesting of former laws into method and order three things are requisite—judgment to know them, art to dispose them, and diligence to omit none of them." If the draftsman has "art to dispose them," if he is something of a stylist, consolidation is his only chance to frame a Bill with a logical layout, putting first things first and next things next. He has not to worry over the hazards and misadventures of controversial debates and divisions as on other occasions. The restriction on the power to amend means that sometimes a doubt has to be consolidated; [25] sometimes also a new lease of life is given to what is ridiculous. The consolidating Solicitors Act of 1932 preserves an old provision which allows a law student, if he fails in his final or intermediate examination, to appeal to the Master of the Rolls "on account of the nature and difficulty of the questions put to him by the examiners." [26] That fanciful provision had to be reproduced; it was on record that one elderly unsuccessful candidate had invoked it; it could not be called obsolete. The object of consolidation is to re-write the law where a principal Act has been frequently amended. Administrative legislation, like State insurance against ill health or unemployment, has been incessantly amended in Britain. Health insurance law, first enacted in 1911, was consolidated in 1924 and again in 1936—not a bad record. Our Ministry of Health has set a good example in this way.

The third and last method of improvement is codification. Whereas consolidation reduces several statutes com-

[25] See Ilbert's interesting example, *The Mechanics of Law Making*, pp. 19–22.

[26] 22 & 23 Geo. 5, c. 37, s. 33.

pendiously into a single new statute, codification reduces all the law, whether contained in statutes or in the common law or in judicial decisions, into a single statute. Jeremy Bentham was the great apostle and prophet of codification. He wanted all the law to be in a code; he wanted nothing to be the law which was not in the code. The very words "codify" and "codification" are his invention. His ideas on the subject were not realized in his lifetime, but the ferment went on working. I have mentioned the historian Macaulay, who went out to India as legal member of the council of the Governor-General of the East India Company. In India he devised a new form of legislative expression in framing what ultimately took shape as the Indian penal code. First he made a clear statement of the leading idea; then he explained any doubtful terms; then he set out any definite exceptions; finally he gave concrete examples. Being Macaulay, he gave a strong literary flavour to these examples; dealing, for instance, with fabrication of false evidence, he gives an illustration which is clearly the story of Lady Macbeth and the grooms.

Sir Frederick Pollock somewhere points out that statute law has a serious defect in that it does not give instances.[27] One sometimes sees statutory expressions which would be much easier to understand if the book had pictures. Sometimes too a blackboard and a bit of chalk would be helpful in exposition. Bentham, I believe, meant his vast code to have a running commentary of

[27] The University Elections (Simple Transferable Vote) Regulations contain illustrative sums; how else could they be understood? See S. R. & O. 1918 (No. 1348) II, 583 (Schedule 1 at p. 589).

reasons and explanations. Bentham's ideas, as I was saying, began to work late in England as also in some of the States of America. In England the authorities were not prepared for a code; they compromised with a digest, a sort of half-way house. Now a digest is merely somebody's idea of the law; it has no more authority than a textbook; the value depends on the author. As Chalmers used to say, there is no *tertium quid* between a textbook and an authoritative statute; the best one can say for a digest is that it is easily turned into a draft code. There is an interesting parallel in the Philadelphia re-statement of the general principles of the common law which, because of the high authority of the American Law Institute, almost takes the place of a code. Nor should we forget the experiment of the Code of the Laws of the United States of America which has been in force since July, 1926. It was not allowed actually to supersede and repeal the previous enactments; it is therefore not the law which later statutes amend.

In 1866 there was a royal commission in England to inquire into the expediency, not of a code, but of a digest. Stephen, who had been out in India where much codification had been done, came back to England in 1872 with hopes of codifying at home. He made a digest of the law of evidence, and he framed a draft penal code. The code was, as Chalmers used to say, lost in an Irish storm in Grand Committee in the Commons. Codification thus had a setback until Sir Frederick Pollock, consciously following Macaulay and Stephen, made a digest of the law of partnership and later turned the digest into a code. Sir Mackenzie Chalmers made a digest of the law of cheques and negotiable instruments and turned this too into a code. Chalmers' Bills of Exchange Act became law in 1882, Pollock's Partnership Act became law in 1890.[28] Both were the result of private enterprise; the Institute of Bankers was interested and backed them. Chalmers also codified the law of sale of goods and the law of marine insurance; these were passed into law in 1893 and 1906, respectively.[29] He used to say that, if there were twenty-five hundred leading cases on—say—negotiable instruments, you could reckon the cost at £100 each and it made a big total. Codification was cheaper than litigation. Judicial decision meant putting new wine into old bottles; codification meant putting old wine into new bottles. Which, he would ask, is the better plan? He maintained that experience showed that, if the mercantile community wanted such codes, the legislature would not stand in the way; but the initiative must come from outside the legislature.

> Politicians naturally take no interest in non-party measures backed by no outside pressure, and lawyers as a rule look on codification with the same pious shrinking as that with which an orthodox doctor would regard a medical prescription written in English instead of in dog Latin.

These four codes in the field of commercial law were a piece-meal effort, soon spent. Broad schemes of a general code have long been in abeyance. Lord Bryce, the first Carpentier lecturer, has written that Justinian's plan

[28] 45 & 46 Vict. c. 61; 53 & 54 Vict. c. 39.
[29] 56 & 57 Vict. c. 71; 6 Edw. 7, c. 41.

for arranging and consolidating the law (completed in six years—"too short a time for so great a work") was due to the profusion with which Diocletian and his successors had used their legislative power, flooding the Empire with a mass of ordinances "which few persons could procure or master." If in Justinian the philosophic theory (such as Plato might have wished to see enthroned in the seat of power) had an exceptional chance to make permanently important changes by a few sweeping measures, "theory might have failed if it had not been reinforced by the vanity of an autocrat who desired to leave behind him an enduring monument." Napoleon's code, based on the Roman law, already in part codified under Louis XIV, was "a step so bold that it could hardly have been attempted except by an autocrat and on the morrow of a revolution." In Germany the general code was a symptom of national unity.

There seems no reason why clear re-statement of the law should be possible only in countries like Justinian's Rome or Napoleon's France where an autocrat can order experts to get on with it. The common-law countries are not, I think, convinced that codification will give the clarity and simplicity we desire. The statutory consolidation of the laws of the City of New York, aided in no small degree by expert help from Columbia University, shows what can be done. In England separate branches of the criminal law have been re-written. The unfortunate fate of the income-tax consolidation has been discouraging; but the tidying up of statutes covering many subjects of administrative law has also initiated legislation prescribing that certain ranges of by-laws made by local authorities shall lapse after ten years, thus ensuring periodical reconsideration.

However intermittently applied, these three processes of expurgation, consolidation, and codification have done much to compress the bulk and modernize the language of the British statute-book. A fourth process has recently been evolved for improving its substance of the law. The Lord Chancellor has appointed a body of experts consisting of judges, practising lawyers, and academic lawyers, known as the Law Revision Committee. This body is asked to examine specific legal tangles created by the trend of judicial decisions or otherwise. It suggests amendments, and in several cases legislation has been passed to give effect to the suggestions. Thus the old rule that a personal action dies with the person has been abolished in England; it is no longer cheaper for the motorist to kill his pedestrian than merely to injure him. Husbands are no longer liable to pay damages for defamatory remarks made by their wives. Dean Young Smith is, I know, working on a similar Law Revision Committee for New York. This revision of the substance of the law is mainly devoted to revising doctrines of common law and equity, not to revising statute law. Perhaps some day, when common law and equity have been dealt with, the Law Revision Committee's beneficent activities might be diverted to the statutes. A clear re-statement of the law of distress, for instance, would be useful in England. Some of the statutes on the subject are among the very earliest in our statute-book.

The remedy, you see, is legislation and more legislation. There is no great objection to this. According to Zenophon someone once remarked to Socrates that laws were not of much account when the very men who passed them would presently be repealing and amending them. Well, said Socrates, States often make peace after going to war: you wouldn't scold those who behave well in war-time on the ground that peace may be made some day. For legislation, however, there is neither time nor enthusiasm. Some of the topics are thorny. When he lectured here in 1913, Sir Courtenay Ilbert mentioned some which it would be imprudent to touch—enactments intended to restrict or to destroy the powers of the Pope in Britain in Tudor times and earlier, for fear of incurring the anathemas of ecclesiastical lawyers. Times are changing, and it would be possible now to propose the repeal of some of these. But there remains a strong sentimental attachment to what is old. In 1938 outlawry proceedings were at last abolished in England. There had been no case of outlawry for a long time, and there were not likely to be any more. The draftsman, following the usual and proper technique, not only abolished outlawry proceedings in general terms but he also eliminated all references to outlawry in the statute-book wherever he found them. One such reference occurred in the most famous of enactments—"No freeman shall be taken or imprisoned or be disseised of his freehold or liberties or free customs or be outlawed or exiled or any other wise destroyed . . ."—the beginning of that article in Magna Carta which declares that no man shall be condemned but by lawful judgment of his peers or by the law of the land. The draftsman proposed to repeal those words "outlawed or." Somebody noticed it and raised the flag of liberty. It was true that nobody could in future be outlawed, and the words were thus unnecessary; but it was no time to be tampering with Magna Carta. The Bill was amended, and the words were preserved.[30]

With this whimsical blend of history and sentiment an insular people cherishes the tattered banners of ancient struggles for civic freedom—the show of House of Commons independence in introducing at the beginning of each session the Bill for the Suppression of Clandestine Outlawries (in spite of outlawry having now been abolished), the fiction of the Stewardship of the Chiltern Hundreds, the pretence that it would not be safe to have a permanent Army Act, the pause of the monarch before crossing the boundary of the City of London. Somehow they are linked with other colourful bits of pageantry, Their Majesties' golden coach in ceremonial procession, the searching of the vaults of Parliament by the beefeaters, the wigs and robes of the judges, or the ritual of Le Roy le Veult. Touch one of these anachronisms and the islander's inherited memories make him anxious for the safety of other venerated symbols. If for these reasons we must not expect him to blaze with ardour for the modernizing and the orderly re-writing of the laws, ought we not still to pursue the ideal of interesting and instructing him in the legislation for which he is himself in theory responsible? It is too bad to leave him to find it out in the police-court.

[30] House of Commons Debates, 1938, May 9, cols. 1329, 1359, 1360, 1371–73, 1377; House of Lords Debates, 1938, July 25, col. 1119.

6. Bureaucracy

Three major calamities, fire, flood and officials.—BURMESE PROVERB

BACON, in the *Advancement of Learning,* complains that universities and colleges have been dedicated too much to "professory learning." Princes, he says, when they make choice of ministers fit for the affairs of State, find about them "such a marvellous solitude of able men" because there is no collegiate education for the purpose of producing men fit for the public service. If we turn from his times to what in England today we call the "civil service," a career service recruited by competitive examination, what education ought a civil servant to have? Ought it to be broad and unspecialized, as in Britain, or concentrated on administrative subjects, as is sometimes advised in America, where there is so much more "collegiate education" for the purpose? In Britain we have few specialized courses for preparing men and women for an administrative career; nor does the young entrant into the civil service spend his afternoons (as it has been suggested that he should) in attending lectures at some official training college adjacent to Whitehall. He just sits down and tackles such jobs as are entrusted to him; he learns by a sort of apprenticeship. Doubtless it was always so. Henry VIII personally corrected the drafts submitted by his secretaries and is said to have told one of them not to take it amiss. "It is I," said Henry, "that made Cromwell and Wriothesley and Pagett good secretaries, and so must I do to thee." [1] That is the method of trial and error, or progress by catastrophe.

A little general education will do no harm. Chadwick, whom we have already described as a bureaucrat,[2] had some comments to make when in 1853 the Civil Service Commission issued the report which was to give Britain a system of appointment by competitive examination. Some of the young men appointed under the system of patronage, he said, could not read or write, though coming from respectable families; one of them could not number the pages of a document if they exceeded ten.[3] The commission's scheme and educational improvements have had their effect, but we must not look for any special charm of style in the official minutes written on Constitution Avenue or in Whitehall, even though, by what is presumably an accident, there have been public servants like Chaucer, Milton, Dryden, and Marvell, who were literary as well as literate. Bureaucrats develop a language of their own. Mr. Winston Churchill not long ago asked the heads of government departments in London to discourage the prolixity and circumlocution of official notes ("It is also of importance to bear in mind the following considerations" and all that) and the woolly phrases which accompany woolly thinking.[4] For the language of legislation something more formal than conversational speech is fitting, but the pitfalls of pompous-

1 Conyers Read, Mr. Secretary Walsingham (1925), I, 439.

2 See pp. 1 ff., above.

3 Cited by Mr. R. Moses, *The Civil Service of Great Britain* (1914), pp. 27–28.

4 See the London *Times*, August 21, 1940.

ness are everywhere. Stylists admonish us to use the shorter rather than the longer word; they deprecate words of Latin origin, although, when it is the lawmaker who speaks, they might make an exception for the language of Justinian. Public health regulations in Britain use the deplorable expression "deratization," meaning getting rid of rats from ships or buildings. "De-ratting" or "disratting" would have been better, but the influence of a French original in an international convention was too strong. The British public talks about the "black-out"; legislation like the Defence Act has preferred "obscuration of light." The statute-book has accepted "camouflage." The arrangements for shifting population from areas exposed to aerial attack are called "evacuation"; officials even speak of "self-evacuation" and of "evacuees." Mr. A. P. Herbert, M. P., a vigilant critic, suggested "scattering" and "scatterees"; these do not quite convey the exact shade of meaning; somebody wrote in a London newspaper that in his village the immigrant children were happily known as "dumplings." Human speech has its limits and needs its improvisations.

Public documents are a fit occasion for dignified expression. Perhaps we have lost the knack of it. We miss today the leisurely accumulation of pleonasms which adorn a Tudor statute. Listen to the preamble of this Act for the attainder of Seymour: [5]

> Not having God before his eyes nor being content with his honourable estate and condition . . . but replenished and filled with the most dangerous, insatiable and fearful vice of

[5] 2 & 3 Edw. 6, c. 18.

ambition and greediness of rule, authority and dominion . . . did determine and resolve . . .

and so forth. The draftsman piles up his phrases—"crafty and subtle," "devise and imagine," "hinder and let," "realms and dominions," "power and authority," "faction and confederation," "compass and devise," "full accompt and rendering," "traitorous intent and purpose." Somehow it fits; he was not writing a telegram. The Hanoverians descend to the bathos of such a recital as this: "Whereas the punishment of public whipping of female offenders has been found inexpedient . . ."[6] More inspiring is the preamble to the Naval Discipline Act:

> Whereas it is expedient to amend the law relating to the government of the Navy, whereon, under the good providence of God, the wealth, safety, and strength of the Kingdom chiefly depend.

The callous hand of statute law revision repealed these pious and stately words (presumably *per incuriam*) in 1893, but they were happily restored in 1915.[7]

This matter of official speech is no negligible part of the art of government. The bureaucrat must learn to use language as a conciliatory or tendentious instrument of policy. He can choose a title for his proposed legislation which will be alluring rather than repellent. In England the relief of the poor is now called "public assistance" in order to eliminate any supposed taint of poverty. By authority of statute what we once called a

[6] 57 Geo. 3, c. 75.

[7] 29 & 30 Vict. c. 109: see 5 & 6 Geo. 5, c. 30, s. 15.

"pauper lunatic" must now be called a "rate-aided person of unsound mind"; a "lunatic asylum" is now a "mental hospital."[8] These official euphemisms about lunacy are part of a deliberate plan for persuading the public that mental ill-health can and should obtain expert and sympathetic treatment at the earliest possible moment like any other form of disease.

From this excursus into philology let me return to the theme of bureaucracy. Maybe it is not for those who are themselves civil servants, even if their duties are not executive or "policy-determining," to discuss it. What they say must be discounted. To them the word "bureaucrat" is merely the bad name given to the poor dog before hanging him. To them the usual criticism of administrators playfully or seriously described as bureaucrats is self-destructive. Sloth, for instance, may be one of the seven deadly accusations. A wit said long ago of the civil servants in Whitehall that, like the fountains in Trafalgar Square hard by, they play from ten to four. Sydney Smith's old-fashioned comment on the proposal that the Secretary of State should appoint prison inspectors was that the persons appointed would be sure of a good salary, would be chosen from among the Treasury retainers, and would never go near a prison. But from other critics the charge is one of excessive activity; civil servants are too busy; they will not let things or people alone.

Then on one side it is complained that they fail to think ahead. Sir Henry Taylor, a minor poet and a mod-

[8] 20 & 21 Geo. 5, c. 23, s. 20; 21 & 22 Geo. 5, c. 14, s. 6, sch. 2.

est sort of Machiavelli, wrote a little book called *The Statesman* which, while giving young men some sage advice about a civil career (including the right age to marry and the right sort of wife to choose), advocated the creation of a planning staff a hundred years ago. But on the other side the business man protests that the civil servants get nowhere because their eyes are on the distant horizon; they want to contemplate all conceivable contingencies. He will tell you that the country cannot start a new munition factory without some cautious official wanting to consult the Ministry of Agriculture about the existing use of the site, the Ministry of Transport about the access and communications, and the Ministry of Health about the water supply, sanitation, and housing accommodation. Precautions, according to a dictum attributed to Captain Cook, are always blamed; whenever they are successful they are said to be unnecessary. If there has been no such consultation, the newspaper columns will mark the omission.

The contrast between the conditions of public service and of private enterprise is familiar. The two seem to be more closely assimilated in the United States than in Britain. In local government America knows the town manager and even, in rare cases, the county manager. Britain has no such officer, except that official nominees were temporarily substituted for defaulting boards of guardians in certain English boroughs in 1926, owing to difficulties with poor relief and finance.[9] The affairs

[9] See 16 & 17 Geo. 5, c. 20 (now superseded), and 19 & 20 Geo. 5, c. 17, s. 20.

of an English town or county are administered, as we have already seen, by a system of committees and expert advisers. In the larger field of national administration the appointment of a general manager to a governmental agency would probably excite less surprise in America than in Britain, where the direction is in the hands of trained civil servants. The latter are, in the nature of things, more cautious than the business man. They carry out the policy of a minister responsible to Parliament; and so, as one of the shrewdest observers of Whitehall remarked to the Committee on Ministers' Powers, "your civil servant is a timorous fowl; the last thing he wants is to get his minister into trouble." Lord Stamp has explained that it is not quite fair to scold government employees for being careful where the business man can be bold. In commerce and industry the young man is encouraged to go ahead and risk making mistakes. Private undertakings can prosper in that way; they can press forward here and draw back there as opportunities offer, developing a local success and forgetting a local failure. Your civil servant has to treat the whole country alike; his mistakes will not be allowed to sink into oblivion.

To John Stuart Mill, who was emphatic that skilled and trained administrators were wanted for government, the most fatal vice of bureaucrats was routine. The red tape with which they tie their papers has become a symbol; some years ago in England white tape was substituted to encourage a new spirit in Whitehall. Something can perhaps be done to lever officials out of their grooves by transferring them to other duties from time to time. These plants are the better for periodical re-potting. Mr. Harold Laski has elaborated Mill's indictment.[10] When the civil servant attains seniority, he says, he becomes habituated to a routine of thought which deprecates innovations. The system produces a public servant "with no imagination in opening out new lines of state policy which are of increasing importance." Any large-scale innovation is "ably and pertinaciously resisted" from within the civil service, which is "very nearly the perfect instrument for the negative State." And that, says Mr. Laski, is what a reforming President of the United States who abolished the patronage system would have to look out for. He considers that there was more of the vital qualities of inventiveness and risk-taking in Washington under the New Deal than there has been in Whitehall for a generation. The permanent non-political official cannot, of course, initiate revolutionary policies. There must first be an effective majority in the legislature in favour of large-scale innovation and a political chief who will tell his department what the policy is to be. To Palmerston in 1838 bureaucratic government meant that the management of routine by permanent subordinates gave them the power of directing policy; the long experience of what had been done in former times and the knowledge of the easiest means of doing what was required in the present time gave them an advantage over political chiefs whose tenure of office was transitory.[11] Political heads of departments in England

[10] *The American Presidency*, p. 221.

[11] *Letters of Queen Victoria, 1837 to 1861*, I, 137.

might claim it to be their function to tell the permanent officials how much the country will stand. It is true on the one hand that almost all the legislation is initiated by the departments in Whitehall, though latterly some striking personal successes have been won by private members of Parliament—by Mr. A. P. Herbert, for example, with his Matrimonial Causes Act, 1937, Miss Ellen Wilkinson with her Hire-Purchase Act, 1938, and Miss Eleanor Rathbone with her Inheritance (Family Provision) Act, 1938. It is true, on the other hand, that the permanent official in peace-time finds ample opportunity for discouraging impulsive proposals; many reformers have a pathetic belief in a new statute as a panacea for every human ill; it may be a duty to marshal the second thoughts and to use the traditional formula of obstructionists "Reform, certainly, but not this particular reform." If, it is said, a bureaucrat wants to damn a proposal, he calls it academic. His approach to politics is empirical; he handles each question on its merits, is guided by precedent and instinct; he is bound up with the existing order, the maintenance of tradition and the "safe" line. And so he easily degenerates into the mandarin.[12]

Bagehot's conception of bureaucrats was that they tended to hate the rude untrained public, to think them stupid, ignorant, and reckless, to feel that the public did not know its own interest and ought to have the leave of the office before it did anything. He notes that the Americans have tried to get on not only with changing heads to

[12] Professor E. Hallett Carr, *Twenty Years' Crisis* (1940), p. 22.

a bureaucracy but also without any stable bureaucracy at all.

> They have facilities for trying it which no one else has. All Americans can administer, and the number of them really fit to be in succession lawyers, financiers or military managers is wonderful.

Americans, he says, need not fear a change of all their officials as a European country would fear it, because all the incoming substitutes are sure to be much better than in Europe; moreover, there is no fear in America, as there is in England, that the outgoing officials will be left destitute in middle life with no hope for the future and no recompense for the past—because in America (whatever the reason for it) there are countless opportunities, and a man who is ruined by being "off the rails" in England in America soon gets on to another line.

Bagehot was writing in 1867, before any movement for a permanent service had begun in America. If that movement starts with the lower ranks of officialdom and works upwards, it has the support of Aristotle, who advised that the smaller posts should be held on a long tenure, but the more important, assigned to the few, should be of brief duration because nobody should be raised to a disproportionate height for more than a short time.[13] Mr. Robert Moses has noted that there was not in England, as in many of the United States, any reasoned principle of rotation of appointments. If in America rotation hindered sound and stable government, in England (where the party in power may have to resign on a defeat in the

[13] *Politics*, V, vii.

House of Commons) it would have stopped government altogether.

> With a tenure of at least four years and probably at least four more, the United States could survive rotation though the troubles of appointment might kill the President; but no English cabinet could maintain itself in office a single year supported at Whitehall by an untrained rabble without certain tenure and opposed in Parliament at every turn by an embittered and rapacious minority. Who would form a cabinet under such circumstances? Who would care to enter the civil service with so hazardous a tenure? [14]

Mr. Moses has painted the popular idea of the bureaucrat—"a stout fierce man in uniform who pries into your private business, insults you and threatens to report you to a fiercer man in a finer uniform who will put you to death." [15] Certainly the putting on of uniform invests a man with a different personality. Yet tradition and training can ensure that the uniformed policeman is not always fierce nor the omnibus drivers and conductors impatient or discourteous. Bad manners are an avoidable cause of offence on the part of bureaucrats. Bentham in his *Constitutional Code* finds a place for Rules of Official Deportment, which, he says, are broadly such rules of good behaviour, good breeding, and decorum as apply. He had, by the way, rather a fondness for that phrase which appears in the disciplinary code of the British army, "behaving in a scandalous manner unbecoming the conduct of an officer and a gentleman." [16] His

[14] *The Civil Service of Great Britain* (1914), p. 25.
[15] *Ibidem*, p. 265.
[16] See Bentham's *Works* (Bowring's edition), IX, 308.

plausible suggestions for "giving satisfaction to aggrieved citizens" (he is thinking perhaps mainly of the official sins of oppression and extortion, but he mentions also "needless and ungrounded contempt or disrespect") include a Public Opinion Tribunal [17] and a system of appeals which seems to be the earliest English plan for administrative courts.[18] He offers a right of appeal to the head of the department and thence possibly to the Prime Minister. His device of placing a complaint-book in the audience chambers of public offices, so that the irritated citizens can vent their annoyance, might be worth trying.

A clause in the English law governing the accounts and audit of local authorities concedes to anybody who is aggrieved the right to a personal hearing (short of a public inquiry) by a person appointed for the purpose by the Minister of Health.[19] This is the kind of civil attention that a business firm would not deny to a customer. The business house can adopt the attitude that the customer is always right; the official may be obliged to make a stand against recalcitrant citizens, though even so the velvet glove may be worn over the iron hand. Plato says that there are two ways of obtaining obedience to the law—one penal, the other persuasive—and that the second is too rarely tried. A well-phrased exhortation to the British tax-payer, extracted from a Parliamentary speech of the Chancellor of the Exchequer, was circulated with the income-tax demands not long ago; it had admirable

[17] *Ibidem,* pp. 41, 157.

[18] *Ibidem,* IX, s. 20. See H. W. Arndt, *Journal of Comparative Legislation* (1939), XXI, 198.

[19] 23 & 24 Geo. 5, c. 51, s. 231(2).

results. On September 28, 1938, when the mobilization of the British fleet put a severe strain on the telephone service, the Postmaster-General appealed to telephone subscribers to restrict non-essential conversations to the minimum. The appeal was repeated next day. On the thirtieth he thanked everybody for the response. Polite explanations and advice from the policeman to the motorist have been worth while. Tact indeed is needed. The Ministry of Food, when granting permits for additional sugar to housewives for making marmalade at home, reserved a right to see that the sugar had been used for the proper purpose. The newspapers reported the various reactions to this condition. One housewife tore up the permit and sent back the pieces; she was not accustomed to having her word doubted or her premises inspected; she would order marmalade from the stores instead, and she was writing a protest to her member of Parliament. Another in the same street, after a polite message of thanks to the Ministry, named her breakfast hour in case the inspector cared to come and taste her handiwork. It takes all sorts to make a world.

These are trivialities. The major sins imputed to the civil service by Sir Gregory Hardlines in Trollope's novel *The Three Clerks* are idleness, incompetence, and dishonesty. The service, said Sir Gregory, contains the family fools of the aristocracy and the middle classes and has become a hospital for incurables and idiots. Trollope has confessed that he drew this character on the lines of Sir Charles Trevelyan, whose system of competitive examination the novelist disfavoured. The story was published in 1858; even then the lines must have been much too hard to be true. Severe things are doubtless still said of civil servants. If they should not be entirely deserved, it may be submitted that to hold the service up to contempt and ridicule is not the ideal way of persuading the best young men in the country to enter it. The work is greater than the official; it masters him and gives him a sense of responsibility. Samuel Pepys found himself appointed to the Navy Office and at first had so little interest in the post that he thought of selling it. Knowing nothing previously of ships and the sea, he nevertheless did his work with much more industry and not much worse corruption than the times expected of him. Many of the sins of bureaucrats may be forgiven if they can reach his standard. *The Three Clerks,* you remember, contains the classic example of a civil servant's lapse into crime. Alaric Tudor, one of the three, a young man with more ability than principle, is sent down to Devonshire with Mr. Fidus Neverbend, who, with a name like that, is of course an uncompromising example of rectitude. Their official mission is to settle some dispute about the boundaries of a mine situated on Crown property. He goes out at night to meet a friend, in spite of Mr. Neverbend's advice. Regardless of the principles of natural justice and forgetting that he is a member of an administrative tribunal, he finds himself buying shares in the mine; he then writes a report which sends the shares soaring upwards. He makes other investments and fortunately (for him, but not for her) becomes trustee of a rich young woman with £20,000. Having used her money to pay the calls on his shares, he is sent to prison for embezzlement, comes out, and goes off to make a fresh start in Australia.

Disputes between the public and the bureaucrats in the field of administrative law make work for the numerous and growing band of official lawyers. Fifty years ago in Britain the Treasury Solicitor employed firms of private practitioners to undertake his litigation on behalf of departments; nowadays he and his large staff attend to it themselves. There seems to be a growing demand for law-trained personnel in the government service. The lawyer is far more valuable to that service if he has had practical experience of ordinary professional work. Conversely it has been observed in the United States that government service has been the school in which many distinguished lawyers (and not a few great advocates) received the training which made them attractive to the large organizations of which they afterwards became members. The teams of legal advisers to the various ministries in Britain form a caste with a tradition which harmonizes loyalty to the public service with loyalty to the law and its professional ethics. Outside the ranks of these regulars there are other lawyers, whole-time or part-time; to analyse the system of their appointment and the merits of their qualifications one would need to examine each case, man by man, with the method of biographical approach adopted by Mr. Arthur W. Macmahon and Mr. John D. Millett in their study of *Federal Administrators* in 1939. The official lawyer certainly has a part to play in the bureaucratic hierarchy as a buffer between the executive and the law and perhaps even between both of them and the public. If there were any sinister or careless tendency on the part of the executive towards illegality or injustice or impatience with the law, he has the chance and the duty to correct it.[20] His outlook is, or should be, wider than that of the administrators; he will instinctively be thinking what there is to be said on the other side; he will often have to advise whether the department can or cannot take a particular course. His independence is important; subservient advice is useless. If he is concerned with the enforcement of the law, his work will bring him into specially close contact with the public.

The responsibility for prosecutions in the most serious cases rests in England with the Attorney General and the Director of Public Prosecutions, officers of such high standing that their decisions command full confidence; many statutes stipulate that proceedings shall not be initiated without the consent of one or other of them. Inevitably the initiative in enforcing many statutes and regulations and orders will lie with the executive. The element of discretion here needs special vigilance, no matter how high-minded the exercise. A few years ago the Criminal Statistics for England and Wales officially stated that the modern policy is not to take proceedings for attempted suicide unless temporary detention is in

20 See Sir A. H. Dennis, "The Official Lawyer's Place in the Constitution," *Law Quarterly Review*, XLI (1925), 378, and the high claims made for departmental lawyers by Sir Maurice Gwyer in his evidence before the Committee on Ministers' Powers, at p. 2 (par. 7).

the defendant's own interest or for other sufficient reason.[21] This is an admirable and humane practice; but ought not the laws to be altered so as to justify it? We are not afraid of our police in Britain, but we ought not to be giving them even in small matters the dispensing power which we refused to the Stuarts in great. Any suggestion from above that the local justices should be more severe in sentencing persons convicted of particular offences suggests a like danger.

To the famous Unlearned Parliament no lawyer was summoned, but only those known to be ignorant of any course of law. By reason whereof, says Coke, the Parliament was fruitless and never a good law made thereat. The lawyers who advise a department have no share in determining policy, but they do shoulder the burden of formulating its effects upon the public in the shape of rules, regulations, and orders. The more difficult tasks of this kind in England are entrusted to the Parliamentary Counsel to the Treasury, the official draftsmen to whom I have so often referred. Sir Courtenay Ilbert told you of their work in his lectures here in 1913. But, whereas in his time he had but one assistant, with perhaps an extra hand to "devil" the work, as we call it, there are nowadays five official draftsmen and as many more undergoing the necessary apprenticeship. The senior Parliamentary Counsel is one of a team, *primus inter pares;* he does not interfere with his colleagues' labours. The government departments in England constantly consult this office; one of its functions is to clarify

[21] Cmd. 3581 (1928), p. lxviii.

the political or departmental mind by eliciting the exact definition of the policy for which legislation is contemplated. Private members' Bills are usually referred to it for report upon their form and substance. It compiles many valuable memoranda on legislative projects. Many Bills which have been demanded in time past, but which have never had their chance in Parliament, lie in its pigeon-holes, often now so far behind the times that they would need re-writing before being introduced today. One might fairly say of these draftsmen that they are, in fact and of necessity, the key men of Whitehall, the hardest worked, the most severely tried. Having no politics themselves, they have to know every point of Parliamentary procedure, every move in the political game. They could—but you may be sure they will not—tell you the truth about many a famous minister, his strength and his weakness. They must be tactful but firm. They must not interfere with policy, but, because of their experience of obstruction, they can anonymously suggest the best legislative ideas. Their knowledge of law has to be extensive and accurate. Their responsibility is grave; if they make mistakes, the applecart will be upset indeed. On rare occasions the temptation of the politician to excuse himself by throwing the blame on the draftsman suggests that the draftsmen make more mistakes than in fact they do.

I have laboured these references to the English Parliamentary Counsel on this and other occasions because of the interest which Columbia University has taken in that branch of public service which consists of legislative drafting. President Butler's annual report on the University for the year 1937 paid a high and, we know, appropriate tribute to the encouragement of that work by Professor J. P. Chamberlain's foundation of the Legislative Drafting Research Fund. There has been a happy and helpful contact between the university and the Legislative Counsel's Office in Washington, the existence and growth of which is in no small degree due to the interest of the University in public affairs and its policy of encouraging scientific participation in them through its Law and other Faculties.[22] To train men in the interpretation and drafting of statute law, to achieve a more careful preparation of Bills and a more precise use of language, to translate vague political aspirations into sensible and solid form—there are few objects more desirable than these in which academic life and public service can be associated. Austin affirmed that the technical part of legislation was incomparably more difficult than the ethical. Whether that be an over-statement or not, it is one of the foundations of the Rule of Law that the laws should be clear and certain.

The laws, alas, go on multiplying in spite of Maine's observations upon the legislative infertility of democracies. Fresh statutes enlarge the snowball of officialdom. We have come a long way from Herbert Spencer's condemnation of "impatiently agitated schemes for improving our sanitary condition by Act of Parliament." Increase of the duties of the central power, De Tocqueville

[22] See F. P. Lee, "The Office of the Legislative Counsel," *Columbia Law Review*, XXIX (1929), 381.

warned us, involves increase of the number of functionaries. The central agencies of government have not been created on any logical plan. They were called into being as they were wanted—sometimes long after they were wanted. Their organization has been haphazard. Chadwick's General Board of Health was created in England with a discretion to bring special powers into force wherever there was a high death-rate. There was no medical member on the Board, though one was added by the Metropolitan Interments Act in 1850. And so it could be whimsically said that Parliament had appointed three non-medical administrators (two were peers and the third was a barrister) to look after the health of the living, and then, after a year or two of doubtful success, had called in a physician to bury the dead. The historians of public health in Britain have recorded the failure of statutory precautions for prevention of disease to keep pace with what we know of the causes of disease and the failure, too, of officials and authorities to make use of the existing statutes. Has there been too much bureaucracy or too little?

Contemplating democracy in America, De Tocqueville found two things specially to admire in his day. The first was the people's extreme respect for the law. He thought this was due to the fact that they made the law themselves and could change it. "The second thing I envy this people is the ease with which they do without government." [23] In Britain government has been better tolerated, though it still encounters some of the

[23] G. W. Pierson, *Tocqueville and Beaumont in America* (1938), p. 16.

eighteenth-century suspicions. God himself, it is written in *The Patriot King,* is a limited monarch, "limited by the rule which infinite wisdom prescribes to infinite power." Bureaucrats have too little wisdom and too much power. If we can obtain the best men for government, we shall have the best results. But they will still be human and fallible. "Discontent," said Rasselas, "will not always be without reason under the most just and vigilant administration of public affairs."

Appendix

STATUTORY RESULTS OF THE REPORT OF THE COMMITTEE ON MINISTERS' POWERS

ALTHOUGH I have stated (see pp. 29, 55, above) that the recommendations of the committee have received scant attention, there are four points at which their influence is visible.

I. Soon after the publication of the report the Ministry of Health brought forward an important Local Government Bill; this was to replace dozens of old statutes, which contained different provisions for different kinds of local authorities, by one neat new code which substituted uniform provisions applicable to all the authorities in England. There were many occasions of making rules, regulations, and orders in the Bill; the earlier statutes were full of anomalies; there was no common principle. The select committee of Parliament which prepared the Bill took the report of the Committee on Ministers' Powers into account and applied its recommendations to the following extent: (1) all important regulations were to be laid before both Houses with power to annul by adverse resolution; (2) certain orders which under the old laws had to be laid before Parliament were to be excused this step in the new statute "because it is generally agreed that a mere obligation to lay before Parliament without the reservation of Parliamentary power to annul is of little value"; (3) all immunity of orders and regulations from judicial challenge was to be eliminated except (*a*) regulations about the issue of stock (these were to be laid in draft and to require an affirmative resolution of both Houses: they would then be unchallengeable); (*b*) compulsory purchase orders (these were to be challengeable in the High Court by a simple procedure, but for a limited period only); (*c*) charters of incorporation and Privy Council schemes accompanying them (these would be dealt with as under the previous law).

II. The committee considered that the nomenclature of delegated legislation should discriminate more carefully between the terms "rules," "regulations," and "orders." This was borne in mind in the consolidating Food and Drugs Act, 1938 (1 & 2 Geo. 6, c. 56). Section 20 authorizes the making of "Milk and Dairies Regulations," whereas the previous law had described them as "Milk and Dairies Orders."

III. The suggestion that reasons should be given in administrative decisions was followed in section 7 (4) of the Restriction of Ribbon Development Act, 1935 (25 & 26 Geo. 5, c. 47). Before determining certain appeals the minister is to hold a public local inquiry and, in giving his decision, he is to "publish a summary of the facts as found by him and of his reasons for the decision."

IV. The committee echoed a recommendation, which other committees had already made in the interests of expediting the business of the courts, that the procedure under the prerogative writs of mandamus, prohibition, and certiorari should be simplified. This was carried out by section 7 of the Administration of Justice (Miscellaneous Provisions) Act, 1938 (1 & 2 Geo. 6, c. 63), whereby, in place of the cumbrous process of the old writs, the judges can now make direct orders.

Index